WHAT IT TAKES TO
WIN

BIBLE STUDY GUIDE

From the Bible-teaching ministry of

Charles R. Swindoll

INSIGHT FOR LIVING

Charles R. Swindoll is a graduate of Dallas Theological Seminary and has served as senior pastor of the First Evangelical Free Church of Fullerton, California, since 1971. Chuck's radio program, "Insight for Living," began in 1979. In addition to his church and radio ministries, Chuck enjoys writing. He has authored numerous books and booklets on a variety of subjects.

Based on the outlines and transcripts of Chuck's sermons, the study guide text is co-authored by Bryce Klabunde, a graduate of Biola University and Dallas Theological Seminary. He also wrote the Living Insights sections.

Editor in Chief:
Cynthia Swindoll

Coauthor of Text:
Bryce Klabunde

Assistant Editor:
Wendy Peterson

Copy Editors:
Deborah Gibbs
Cheryl Gilmore
Glenda Schlahta

Designer:
Gary Lett

Publishing System Specialist:
Bob Haskins

Director, Communications Division:
Deedee Snyder

Manager, Creative Services:
Alene Cooper

Project Supervisor:
Susan Nelson

Print Production Manager:
John Norton

Printer:
Sinclair Printing Company

Unless otherwise identified, all Scripture references are from the New American Standard Bible, © The Lockman Foundation 1960, 1962, 1963, 1968, 1971, 1972, 1973, 1975, 1977. Used by permission. The other translation cited is J.B. Phillips: The New Testament in Modern English [PHILLIPS].

An effort has been made to locate sources and obtain permission where necessary for the quotations used in this book. In the event of any unintentional omission, a modification will gladly be incorporated in future printings.

ISBN 0-8499-8475-0
Printed in the United States of America.

COVER DESIGN: Nina Paris
COVER PHOTOGRAPH: The Bettman Archive

CONTENTS

INTRODUCTION

When was the last time you thought about the rewards God has promised His people?

How about the ministry? Have you ever pondered what it means to minister to others?

And while we are asking questions, does the Great Commission have much to do with today?

All the above directly relate to serving the Lord . . . actually, what it takes to win in this life. My hope is that each one of these studies will probe far beneath the superficial veneer of mere "religious activity" and force us to examine not only our actions but also our motives behind them.

As I put this series of messages together, I had in mind those who may have lost their motivation . . . their determination. If your mind has cooled toward the Lord and your heart has begun to wander, I pray that this study of God's Word will do a permanent work in your life and give you the courage to win.

Chuck Swindoll

Chuck Swindoll

PUTTING TRUTH INTO ACTION

K nowledge apart from application falls short of God's desire for His children. He wants us to apply what we learn so that we will change and grow. This study guide was prepared with these goals in mind. As you go through the following pages, we hope your desire to discover biblical truth will grow as your understanding of God's Word increases, and that you will be encouraged to apply what you've learned.

To assist you in your study, we've included a section called **Living Insights** at the end of each lesson. These exercises will challenge you to study further and to think of specific ways to put your discoveries into action.

There are many ways to use this guide—in personal devotions, group studies, discussions with friends and family, and Sunday school classes. And, of course, it's an ideal study aid when you're listening to its corresponding "Insight for Living" radio series.

To benefit most from this study guide, we would encourage you to consider it a spiritual journal. That's why we've included space in the **Living Insights** for recording your thoughts and discoveries. We hope you'll return to those sections often for review and encouragement as you continue to grow in your walk with Christ.

Bryce Klabunde

Bryce Klabunde
Coauthor of Text
Author of Living Insights

WHAT IT TAKES TO
WIN

OUR ETERNAL GOALS

Chapter 1

A LOOK AT
ALL THE CROWNS

Selected Scriptures

W hat have been some of the most exciting moments in your life? That special Christmas morning you bounded down the stairs to discover the present you'd been dreaming about for months? That magical moment you said, "I do"? Or that miracle of your baby's first cry?

As Christians, we look forward to an even more exciting event—one that will pale all others. It will happen the second we pass through death's shadow into heaven's splendor and see our Lord face-to-face. What will it be like?

> Think of—
> Stepping on shore, and finding it Heaven!
> Of taking hold of a hand, and finding it God's hand.
> Of breathing a new air, and finding it celestial air.
> Of feeling invigorated, and finding it immortality.
> Of passing from storm to tempest to an unbroken
>   calm.
> Of waking up, and finding it Home.[1]

What a thrilling moment! Just thinking about it can make our hearts beat faster. Perhaps, though, it has been a long time since you've imagined your glorious future—what with the household

---

1. "Heaven," author unknown, in *Poems That Live Forever*, comp. Hazel Felleman (New York, N.Y.: Doubleday, 1965), p. 331. A version of this poem has also appeared under the title "The Homeland," attributed to Myrtle Erickson in *Knight's Master Book of New Illustrations*, comp. Walter B. Knight (1956; reprint, Grand Rapids, Mich.: William B. Eerdmans Publishing Co., 1987), p. 279.

chores and the bills and the car repairs and the sick kids and . . . does the list ever end? In our hectic lives, we need an "encouragement break" from time to time. That's what this first section of our study guide is designed to give you.

Sadly, though, when the idea of facing Jesus comes up, many of us are filled more with dread than encouragement. We picture ourselves before an immense, compassionless throne, shaking and quivering in our guilt and imperfections while God replays a video of our lives and points out every flaw and failure.

But Jesus said that He will come quickly with a reward—not a club—in His hand (Rev. 22:12). Judgment is past for Christians, as John and Paul and Jude jubilantly exclaim throughout the New Testament![2] So let's study and ask questions and find answers that will dispel our fears and bring the sureness of our joy into focus.

Why Is It Helpful to Know about Eternal Rewards?

Awareness of our eternal rewards can help us spiritually in several ways. First, *God has revealed them in Scripture so we can build a reservoir of knowledge.* When hard times come, we can dip into this reservoir for a refreshing drink of help and hope.

Second, *understanding rewards encourages us when we feel weary and overlooked.* God has not forgotten the toddler-chasing mother, the overworked pastor, the useless-feeling retiree, nor any of His other frazzled, isolated, or downcast children (see Heb. 6:10). One day, He will reward our faithfulness and vindicate our causes.

Third, *knowing about rewards provides motivation to continue in the service of the King.* We are more willing to make sacrifices when we know they're building toward something. Just as Olympic runners train harder because they can win gold medals, our dream of winning heavenly rewards motivates us to stay on track in the Lord's work.

Fourth, *the truth about rewards is good information to pass along to others who are discouraged.* We give scholarships to hard-working students and bonuses to loyal employees. In the same way, we can brighten the eyes of persevering Christians with God's promise of rewards in heaven.

Getting more curious about these rewards? Let's peer into a couple of Scripture passages to discover some specifics.

---

2. See John 3:17–18; 5:24; 1 John 4:17–18; Romans 8:1; Ephesians 2:4–8; 1 Thessalonians 1:10; Jude 24.

What Scripture Teaches regarding the Time and Place of Rewards

In 1 Corinthians 3, Paul uses a farming metaphor to describe how believers work together in the church—one plants, the other waters, but God causes the growth (see vv. 6–7). The rewards theme then emerges in verse 8:

> Now he who plants and he who waters are one; but each will receive his own reward according to his own labor.

The principle is this: although believers work as a team, God issues rewards individually. The Apostle elaborates on this idea by using an architectural metaphor in the next verses:

> No man can lay a foundation other than the one which is laid, which is Jesus Christ. Now if any man builds upon the foundation with gold, silver, precious stones, wood, hay, straw, each man's work will become evident; for the day will show it, because it is to be revealed with fire; and the fire itself will test the quality of each man's work. (vv. 11–13)

"The quality of each man's work" is what wins the Lord's favor, not the quantity of work. In His eyes, one golden deed done in love outweighs a truckload of straw-filled accomplishments. The difference between the two will become clear when the Lord tests our works with fire.

> If any man's work which he has built upon it remains, he shall receive a reward. If any man's work is burned up, he shall suffer loss; but he himself shall be saved, yet so as through fire. (vv. 14–15)

Now rest assured, reward is the subject in these verses, not salvation. Paul is saying that works of quality done with a pure heart will endure; works done from impure motives, however, will burn, causing us to miss out on the rewards we could have received.

Paul again broaches the subject of the believer's rewards in 2 Corinthians 5:1–10. Here he again uses his metaphor of a building, this time to refer to our bodies. He says that although in this life we groan in our wind-torn tents, in the next life we will have solid-wall structures—houses "not made with hands, eternal in the heavens" (v. 1b).

While waiting for our celestial remodeling, though, we must

> have as our ambition, whether at home [with the
> Lord] or absent, to be pleasing to Him. For we must
> all appear before the judgment seat of Christ, that
> each one may be recompensed for his deeds in the
> body, according to what he has done, whether good
> or bad. (vv. 9–10)

"For we must *all* appear . . . that *each one* may be recompensed" (emphasis added). This rewarding of believers is not a group experience—every individual has his or her turn before Christ. At that climactic moment, the Lord will examine, vindicate, and reward each one of us according to our Christian service and deeds, whether large or small, many or few.[3] Paul even specifies the place—the judgment seat, or *bema*, of Christ.

In Greek culture, the *bema* was a judge's platform, often present at an athletic event.[4] According to commentator Joe Wall,

> at the end of the Olympic festival, contestants appeared before the platform of judgment, the *bema*.
> If the judge proclaimed that an individual had won
> and had not been disqualified for some reason, that
> competitor received a crown of olive branches.[5]

Who's our judge? Not our neighbors or pastor or family, but Christ our Savior. He alone knows our motives and can judge us without prejudice or misunderstanding. When will this occur? At some moment after the rapture of the church, as Paul writes in 1 Thessalonians:

> The Lord Himself will descend from heaven with a
> shout, with the voice of the archangel, and with the
> trumpet of God; and the dead in Christ shall rise

---

3. Unlike salvation and spiritual gifts, which are gifts that God freely offers to us even though we do not deserve them (1 Cor. 12:4–7; Eph. 2:8–9), these rewards are earned. God gives them to us in recognition of a job well done.

4. Originally, a *bema* was used in Athens as a platform from which orations were given and, later, as a platform upon which a ruler sat and issued decrees. After battles, Caesars or generals would award crowns of woven branches to heroic soldiers from a *bema*. The word was even used for the platform in synagogues from which the "rabbis pronounced the law, or judgments, of God." Joe L. Wall, *Going for the Gold* (Chicago, Ill.: Moody Press, 1991), p. 32.

5. Wall, *Going for the Gold*, p. 33.

4

first. Then we who are alive and remain shall be caught up together with them in the clouds to meet the Lord in the air, and thus we shall always be with the Lord. (4:16–17)

How exciting! Our bodies—these dilapidated tents we try so hard to prop and patch—will become everlasting houses. In a twinkling, our heavenly life will begin; and in a victory promenade we will pass before the *bema* to receive our long-awaited honor and reward.

Some of the rewards we might receive are called "crowns" in Scripture. Let's take a few moments to survey the five specified in the New Testament.

Which "Crowns" Are Specified in the New Testament?

These five crowns are a special type: the wreath or victor's crown, called *stephanos* in Greek. Another type of crown in the Bible is the *diadēma*, which is "a blue band trimmed with white, on the tiara, hence a symbol of royalty."[6] At the Second Coming, the heavens will open revealing Christ the conquering King, who will be riding a white horse and wearing "many diadems" or many royal headbands (Rev. 19:11–12). That type of crown represents regal supremacy and is reserved for Christ alone.

The *stephanos*, on the other hand, represents worthy service. The Christian may earn different *stephanos* crowns, just as an athlete might win gold medals in different events. Let's bring each one into the spotlight for a moment and see how each is won.

- *The imperishable crown.* For the one who victoriously runs the race of life and "exercises self-control in all things," like a long-distance runner in training, the imperishable crown will be presented (1 Cor. 9:24–25).

- *The crown of exultation or joy.* There is also a crown for those who have declared the gospel to unbelievers, led them to Christ, and built them up as new Christians. These "soul-winners" will receive the crown of exultation or joy (see Phil. 4:1; 1 Thess. 2:19–20).

6. William F. Arndt and F. Wilbur Gingrich, trans., *A Greek-English Lexicon of the New Testament,* by Walter Bauer, 2d ed., rev. and enl., (Chicago, Ill.: University of Chicago Press, 1979), p. 182.

- *The crown of righteousness.* The next crown is reserved for those who, like Paul, have lived for Christ's return and can say, "I have fought the good fight, I have finished the course, I have kept the faith" (2 Tim. 4:7). They will win "the crown of righteousness" (v. 8a).

- *The crown of life.* For the man or woman "who perseveres under trial," Christ will give the "crown of life, which the Lord has promised to those who love Him" (James 1:12).

- *The crown of glory.* Finally, "the unfading crown of glory" will be given to leaders who shepherd God's flock willingly, sacrificially, humbly, and with integrity (see 1 Pet. 5:1–4).

Certainly, heaven alone is reward enough; yet with these crowns, Christ will lavishly heap on us blessing upon blessing. They truly are reason to celebrate and be encouraged—and our joy only deepens when we realize what our crowns cost Him.

One More "Crown" That Makes All the Others Possible

In simple yet somber words, Mark records the brutal crowning of Jesus:

> And the soldiers took Him away into the palace (that is, the Praetorium), and they called together the whole Roman cohort. And they dressed Him up in purple, and after weaving a crown of thorns, they put it on Him; and they began to acclaim Him, "Hail, King of the Jews!" And they kept beating His head with a reed, and spitting at Him, and kneeling and bowing before Him. And after they had mocked Him, they took the purple off Him, and put His garments on Him. And they led Him out to crucify Him. (15:16–20)

This He endured . . . *for us.* How can we thank Him enough? Certainly, our only fitting response in heaven will be the same as the twenty-four heavenly elders—to cast our crowns at His feet and worship the Lamb that was slain.

> The twenty-four elders will fall down before Him who sits on the throne, and will worship Him who lives forever and ever, and will cast their crowns

before the throne. . . .

And I looked, and I heard the voice of many
angels around the throne and the living creatures
and the elders; and the number of them was myriads
of myriads, and thousands of thousands, saying with
a loud voice,

"Worthy is the Lamb that was slain to receive power and riches and wisdom and
might and honor and glory and blessing."

And every created thing which is in heaven and on
the earth and under the earth and on the sea, and
all things in them, I heard saying,

"To Him who sits on the throne, and to the
Lamb, be blessing and honor and glory and
dominion forever and ever." (Rev. 4:10;
5:11–13)

 ## Living Insights

Paul sums up the goal of our studying rewards in the following
verses:

We do not lose heart, but though our outer man
is decaying, yet our inner man is being renewed day
by day. For momentary, light affliction is producing
for us an eternal weight of glory far beyond all com-
parison, while we look not at the things which are
seen, but at the things which are not seen; for the
things which are seen are temporal, but the things
which are not seen are eternal. (2 Cor. 4:16–18)

The Apostle is reminding us to focus on the eternal things,
rather than the temporal, so we can shift our attention from pursuing earthly prizes to accumulating heavenly treasures.

Focusing on eternity is difficult, though, isn't it? Constantly
bearing down on us is our pressing load of worries: the house repairs,
the job demands, the unpaid bills. Add to that the bumps and bruises
of personal relationships, and our hearts often remain earthbound.

Through the Living Insights section of this chapter, let God's
Word bring eternity more into view. Start by meditating on the
previous passage. As you reread it, jot down the words that refer to

7

an earthly perspective and a heavenly perspective. We'll start you off with the first two.

Earthly Perspective	Heavenly Perspective
Outer man	*Inner man*

From the words Paul chose, it is easy to tell what was his focus. Certainly, that heavenly perspective kept his mood steady during difficult days. Do your spirits need lifting? Are the temporal concerns of life overwhelming you? Do you need to restore your sense of purpose and hope? If so, use the following space to release your earthly worries to the Lord, and ask Him to help you, through this study, to pursue heaven's treasures during your time on earth.

_____

_____

_____

_____

_____

_____

Living Insights
STUDY TWO

In his book *Immortality*, Loraine Boettner shares the insightful wit of John Quincy Adams.

> It is said that one day in his eightieth year as he walked slowly along a Boston street he was accosted by a friend who said, "And how is John Quincy Adams today?" The former president of the United States replied graciously, "Thank you, John Quincy Adams is well, sir, quite well, I thank you. But the house in which he lives at present is becoming dilapidated. It is tottering upon the foundations. Time

and the seasons have nearly destroyed it. Its roof is pretty well worn out, its walls are shattered, and it trembles with every wind. The old tenement is becoming almost uninhabitable, and I think John Quincy Adams will have to move out of it soon; but he himself is quite well, sir, quite well." And with that the venerable statesman, leaning heavily upon his cane, continued his slow walk down the street.[7]

What's the condition of your house? Are the joints groaning and creaking a little more? Has harsh weather blown off some rooftop shingles? Or caused a few crack lines? Or produced a slight sag in the middle?

Isn't it wonderful that, according to God's promise, "if the earthly tent which is our house is torn down, we have a building from God, a house not made with hands, eternal in the heavens" (2 Cor. 5:1)?

Take a few moments to look up some other references concerning what is in store for your body, and write down what you discover.

1 Corinthians 15:40–44 _____

_____

1 Corinthians 15:51–54 _____

_____

Philippians 3:20–21 _____

_____

1 John 3:2 _____

_____

Our old houses have quite a remodeling coming up! Next time you look in the mirror, thank the Lord for the gift of your body and for the gift of your glorified body to come. And don't let the sags and wrinkles bother you too much . . . there's still hope!

---

7. Loraine Boettner, *Immortality* (Phillipsburg, N.J.: Presbyterian and Reformed Publishing Co., 1956), p. 29.

Chapter 2

THE IMPERISHABLE CROWN
1 Corinthians 9:19–27

Hours behind the runner in front of him, the last marathoner finally entered the Olympic stadium. By that time, the drama of the day's events was almost over and most of the spectators had gone home. This athlete's story, however, was still being played out.

Limping into the arena, the Tanzanian runner grimaced with every step, his knee bleeding and bandaged from an earlier fall. His ragged appearance immediately caught the attention of the remaining crowd, who cheered him on to the finish line.

Why did he stay in the race? What made him endure his injuries to the end? When asked these questions later, he replied, "My country did not send me 7,000 miles away to start the race. They sent me 7,000 to finish it."[1]

This courageous runner may not have won a medal, but he did finish the race—which is what he was called to do. As God's "runners," that is our goal as well—to finish the race set before us. To bring glory, not shame, to the name of Christ. To discipline ourselves to win. Unlike the runner from Tanzania, though, we *will* receive a reward—the one Paul called the imperishable crown.

Before we examine this first imperishable, or runner's, crown, let's quickly review a few salient points about eternal rewards we learned in our last chapter.

A Brief Review regarding Rewards

First, *all rewards will be given in the future*. Consequently, we must wait for them. Sometimes, though, we forget this and get discouraged, wanting our rewards now. But God distributes very few rewards in this life, and Jesus warned us against seeking earthly laurels:

> "Beware of practicing your righteousness before men to be noticed by them; otherwise you have no reward with your Father who is in heaven." (Matt. 6:1; see also vv. 2, 5, 16)

1. Adapted from "The Marathoner Who Finished Last," *Quote Magazine*, vol. 51, no. 7, July 1991.

After we have been raised from the dead, after we stand before our Lord, then we'll receive the full joy of our rewards.

Second, *no deed worthy of a reward will be overlooked or ignored.* The Lord's faithful, loving eyes see all our God-honoring thoughts, words, and actions, as the writer to the Hebrews affirms:

> God is not unjust so as to forget your work and the love which you have shown toward His name, in having ministered and in still ministering to the saints. (6:10)

Third, *the New Testament teaching on rewards is often related to ancient athletic contests.* Paul especially relayed God's truths through sports imagery, with many of his metaphors coming from the Olympics and Corinth's Isthmian games. Top athletes from all over the Roman Empire would compete in events that included running, leaping, discus throwing, boxing, and wrestling. What a rich field of analogy paraded before Paul, revealing lessons of self-discipline, endurance, concentration, purpose—and reward.

As the victors stood before the judges' *bema*, an official of the Olympic games would place upon their heads an olive wreath—or at the Isthmian games, a pine or wild celery wreath.[2] All that pain, sweat, and sacrifice for a withering wreath! How much better will be the believer's eternal crown.

A Close Look at the "Imperishable Crown"

What does it take to win the imperishable crown? Strict diet and grueling exercise? Not exactly. It does, however, require self-control—a concept embedded in the context of 1 Corinthians 9.

The Overall Context of 1 Corinthians 9

Modeling personal self-control to the Corinthian believers, Paul says,

> Therefore, if food causes my brother to stumble, I will never eat meat again, that I might not cause my brother to stumble. (1 Cor. 8:13)

---

2. After the games, the victor "would normally return to his home city for a hero's welcome. The townspeople, seeking to distinguish him, often would erect a statue in his honor, give him choice seats at public events, and exempt him from taxes." Joe L. Wall, *Going for the Gold* (Chicago, Ill.: Moody Press, 1991), p. 33.

Rather than flaunting his liberty in Christ and telling those less mature to "Deal with it!", Paul respected the sensitivities of the former idol-worshiping Corinthians by refraining from eating the meat sacrificed on idol altars. Out of love, he willingly limited his freedom so that a weaker Christian, who had recently converted to Christ from idolatry, wouldn't stumble (vv. 9–12).

As a further sign of Paul's maturity, he willingly limited other freedoms as well. A minister of the gospel, Paul had certain rights— the right to marry and the right to receive the church's financial support (see 9:5–14). "But," writes the Apostle, "I have used none of these things" (v. 15a).

In fact, concerning his right to financial support, he considered it a reward of love to offer the gospel without charge, "so as not to make full use of my right in the gospel" (v. 18b). He restrained himself so that he "would cause no hindrance to the gospel of Christ" (v. 12b). That takes self-control.

Carrying this principle of restraint to an even higher level, Paul expresses his willingness to forfeit *all* his rights so that others may be saved.

> For though I am free from all men, I have made myself a slave to all, that I might win the more. And to the Jews I became as a Jew, that I might win Jews; to those who are under the Law, as under the Law, though not being myself under the Law, that I might win those who are under the Law; to those who are without law, as without law, though not being without the law of God but under the law of Christ, that I might win those who are without law. To the weak I became weak, that I might win the weak; I have become all things to all men, that I may by all means save some. And I do all things for the sake of the gospel, that I may become a fellow partaker of it. (vv. 19–23)

To save the Jew, the Gentile, or the weak, Paul would consider no demand too strenuous or adaptation too absurd. With the dedicated discipline of an athlete, Paul committed himself to make whatever sacrifices were necessary to win the lost to Christ. And it's to that image of the self-disciplined athlete that he turns next.

The Word Pictures in the Last Four Verses

When Paul was sitting in the grandstands of the games, he probably noted how the runners had their eyes absolutely fixed on their goal—a square pillar at the end of the stadium. As they sprinted, their muscles strained, their legs and arms pumped in perfect rhythm, their necks craned forward as they tried to edge out the opponent and win the race. With this picture in mind, Paul writes:

> Do you not know that those who run in a race all run, but only one receives the prize? Run in such a way that you may win. And everyone who competes in the games exercises self-control in all things. They then do it to receive a perishable wreath, but we an imperishable. (vv. 24–25)

For the spiritual athlete, the goal is the pillar of personal holiness. Reaching the goal requires self-control: the ability to say "no" to temptation, to self-indulgence, to distractions. The prize for such self-discipline is the imperishable crown—the reward Christ will give not just to one victor but to all who pursue holiness with a whole heart . . . who run the race to win.

Admittedly, we often run as if the race were not worth winning. We come to the track half-prepared, still wearing street clothes. When the gun sounds, we jog a few feet then wander over to the snack bar. What kind of race is that? Is that what it takes to win the imperishable crown? No, to win this crown, we must focus our complete effort on pursuing the goal of holiness. We must have the determination of a runner and, according to Paul's next analogy, the aim of a boxer:

> Therefore I run in such a way, as not without aim;
> I box in such a way, as not beating the air. (v. 26)

No good boxer wastes his energy flailing wildly about in the ring; he shrewdly plans his moves so that each punch will land where he wants it. Likewise, Christians are to avoid exhausting themselves on ill-placed jabs. We are to focus on the true contender in our title match with sin—not the enemy without, but the enemy within. This is why Paul writes, "I buffet my body and make it my slave" (v. 27a). Commentator W. Harold Mare elaborates:

> He aims his blows against his own body, beating it

black and blue. . . . The picture is graphic: the ancient boxers devastatingly punishing one another with knuckles bound with leather thongs. And so by pummeling his body, Paul enslaves it in order to gain the Christian prize.[3]

Certainly, Paul is not saying that whenever he speaks angrily or lusts after a woman he gives himself a bloody lip or a black eye. Rather, he jabs his sinful urges and uppercuts his wicked passions as if he were in a boxing match. For he knows the consequence of not subduing his sinful nature—disqualification.

The Warning about Being Disqualified

I buffet my body and make it my slave, lest possibly, after I have preached to others, I myself should be disqualified. (v. 27)

Paul's greatest fear was that, after spurring so many others to victory, he himself should be "disqualified" from receiving his reward. The word is *adokimos* in Greek, which means to be "rejected after testing."[4] For athletes, that testing comes not at the start, when the body is fresh, but toward the end of the contest, when muscles are aching and the mind is tired. The same is true for Christians. When the starting gun sounds at conversion, enthusiasm and confidence are often high; but after many years and miles, weariness and the grind of sin can cause our moral strength to lag and our faith to collapse. Paul, however, determined to make it to the finish line, to fight until the final bell, to end his life strong in the Lord.

A Few Practical Suggestions

What can help us toward a good ending and an imperishable crown? According to Paul, "self-control in all things" (v. 25). As you reflect on your own level of self-control, consider a few practical suggestions that will keep you in the race.

3. W. Harold Mare, "1 Corinthians," in *The Expositor's Bible Commentary*, ed. Frank E. Gaebelein (Grand Rapids, Mich.: Zondervan Publishing House, Regency Reference Library, 1976), vol. 10, p. 246. Interestingly, the word *buffet* is *hupōpiazō*, "to strike under the eye, to beat black and blue." See Fritz Rienecker, *A Linguistic Key to the Greek New Testament*, trans. and ed. Cleon L. Rogers, Jr. (Grand Rapids, Mich.: Zondervan Publishing House, Regency Reference Library, 1980), p. 417.

4. G. Abbott-Smith, *A Manual Greek Lexicon of the New Testament*, 3d ed. (Edinburgh, Scotland: T. and T. Clark, 1937), p. 10.

First, *remember: age works against you*. Young Christians often long for the maturity of age, but many older believers admit that it is actually tougher to walk with Christ as the years increase. For some reason, it just gets easy to take on a business-as-usual attitude with the Lord. The once-thrilling Christian race slows to a jog . . . then a stroll . . . then an afternoon snooze. The apostle Paul, however, was living proof that age does not have to affect the intensity of prayer and worship. An aging, even bedridden, believer can still race to win and, in the end, run to meet the Lord.

Second, *refuse to build a kingdom around your private life*. Kingdoms have castles, and castles have moats and guards to keep people away. We can hide there, safe from hurt or embarrassment. But, ironically, isolating ourselves inhibits our self-control. Instead, we must let down the drawbridge and invite people into our hearts. We must be vulnerable and open to the truth if we are to stay on track spiritually.

Third, *reevaluate your leisure*. What are you reading? What are you watching? What are you fantasizing? These can be difficult questions to face, but they're necessary, because leisure is often the area Satan targets to distract us from the race. Instead, how can your leisure build vivacity into your walk with Christ?

Fourth, *repeat your commitments annually*. If you're married, repeat your wedding vows to your spouse every year. If you volunteer for a position at church or in the community, restate those commitments. Renew your promises to your family and your friends. Above all, repeat your commitment to the Lord. For it is the faith in Christ that started you in the race that will keep you running all the way to the finish line.

Living Insights STUDY ONE

Christ is our model of holy living, our pillar on which we fix our eyes and run toward with all our might. More than anything else, God wants us to become like His Son.

In his book *Growing More Like Jesus*, Richard L. Strauss comments:

> [God] isn't trying to make us successful business people so we can impress the world with our money and affluence. He isn't trying to make us successful

churchmen, so we can amaze people with our organizational and administrative skills. He isn't trying to make us great orators, so we can overwhelm audiences with our persuasive words. He wants to reproduce in us the character of Christ—His love, His kindness, His compassion, His holiness, His humility, His unselfishness, His servant's spirit, His willingness to suffer wrongfully, His willingness to forgive. His character in us is what will attract the world to Him.[5]

On what have your eyes been fixed lately? What has been the focus of your attention and efforts?

- ❏ Career
- ❏ Church
- ❏ Family relationships
- ❏ Friendships
- ❏ Finances

- ❏ Recreation
- ❏ Health
- ❏ School
- ❏ Clothing
- ❏ Raising children

None of these pursuits are wrong in themselves, yet each one has the potential to sidetrack us from our singular goal—to become like Christ. In order to stay in the race, we must angle the different pathways of our lives so they lead us to Christ. The following diagram illustrates our point.

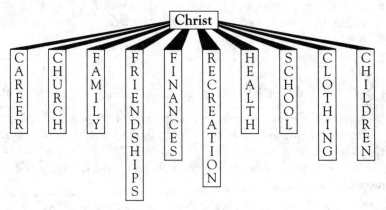

5. Richard L. Strauss, *Growing More Like Jesus* (Neptune, N.J.: Loizeaux Brothers, 1991), p. 17.

In our careers, we can emulate Christ's integrity and honesty. In our churches, we can exemplify Christ's compassion and servant-hood. In our families, we can be modeling Christ's love and joy. And so on. As you reflect on the different directions your life takes you this week, how can you direct them so they keep you in the race toward a Christlike character?

_____

_____

_____

_____

Living Insights

Marathon runners like to race in groups. A lone runner tends to lose his or her sense of time and distance, but two runners can pace each other, keeping one another focused on the race.

The same is true for believers. In our spiritual endurance race, if we run on our own, we lose our direction, our minds stray, and our spirits weaken. So God desires that we pace and challenge one another in our race toward the imperishable crown. Take a moment to look up the following verses, and write down some of the advantages of togetherness in the race of life.

Proverbs 27:17 _____

Galatians 6:1–2 _____

Hebrews 10:23–25 _____

James 5:16 _____

Do you have a running partner? Someone with whom you can be completely honest and vulnerable? If not, who can that person or group of people be? Go ahead—make some contacts, place a few phone calls, and arrange to meet for prayer and support.[6]

---

6. We recommend the following books on the subject of Christian partnership and account-ability: *Intimacy: The Longing of Every Human Heart*, by Terry Hershey (Eugene, Oreg.: Harvest House Publishers, 1984); and *Among Friends*, by James Hinkle and Tim Woodroof (Colorado Springs, Colo.: NavPress, 1989).

Chapter 3

THE CROWN OF EXULTATION

Philippians 4:1; 1 Thessalonians 2:19–20; Acts 8:26–38

Sweeping aside the privacy curtain, the nurse darted out of the hospital room, called a few instructions to another nurse, and ducked back in, replacing the curtain with a jerk. Down the hall a group of family members anxiously watched her every move, then heard a voice mechanically drone over the PA system: "Doctor Miller, Doctor Stanford Miller, please report to Maternity."

Looking up from her cross-stitching, the grandmother caught the mother's eye and grinned, "Doctors are never there when you need 'em. When you were born, there wasn't a doctor within twenty miles. Aunt Berle had to help deliver you; your father just paced like a nervous cat."

In a few moments, a man with a stethoscope draped around his neck rushed by and disappeared into the room.

"See," said Grandma, returning to her stitchery, "everything's gonna be fine."

The mother fingered the wadded tissue in her hand. She pictured her daughter as a little girl, knock-kneed and pigtailed. Now her baby was having a baby! Dabbing her eyes with the tissue, she whispered a prayer.

Then she faintly heard something. Could it be? The other family members glanced at each other for confirmation. They had heard it too. Again it came floating down the hall—that miraculous, choking newborn cry. They all stood up, hoping to hear more as they peered toward the room. Then out came a pale young man— "It's a boy!" the new father beamed. The family cheered and hugged one another, reveling in the joy of the moment.

What emotion can surpass the wonder and elation of a new birth? Certainly, it is one of the richest joys in life. But imagine experiencing that joy for eternity! That's what it will be like to receive from Christ the third crown in our list of five, for this is the crown given to the spiritual parents of newborn believers. It is the soul-winner's crown—the crown of exultation, the crown of joy.

Where the "Crown" Is Mentioned

Paul spiritually parented hundreds of newborn believers during his ministry, and in two of his epistles, he remarked that they were his crown of joy. In his letter to the Philippians, he refers to them as his crown in the context of some thoughts about heaven.

> For our citizenship is in heaven, from which also we eagerly wait for a Savior, the Lord Jesus Christ; who will transform the body of our humble state into conformity with the body of His glory, by the exertion of the power that He has even to subject all things to Himself.
>
> Therefore, my beloved brethren whom I long to see, my joy and crown, so stand firm in the Lord, my beloved. (3:20–4:1)

William Barclay comments on this crown, or *stephanos*, reminding us of this Greek word's significance.

> The word used here . . . has two backgrounds. (i) It was the crown of the victorious athlete at the Greek games. . . . (ii) It was the crown with which guests were crowned when they sat at a banquet, at some time of great joy. It is as if Paul said that the Philippians were the crown of all his toil; it is as if he said that at the final banquet of God they were his festal crown. There is no joy in the world like bringing another soul to Jesus Christ.[1]

It was by a river that Paul witnessed to the first of the Philippians to be born into God's family—Lydia (Acts 16:11–15). Those in her household became Christians, then many others in the city did too—including the jailer who had put Paul and his companion Silas in the stocks (vv. 23–34). Of these men, women, and children, Paul says, "You are my festal crown."

Also crowning Paul with joy were the Thessalonian believers, whom he introduced to Christ. Utilizing the local synagogue as his platform, he proclaimed the gospel for three Sabbaths, until

> some of them were persuaded and joined Paul and Silas, along with a great multitude of the God-fearing Greeks and a number of the leading women. (17:4)

---

1. William Barclay, *The Letters to the Philippians, Colossians, and Thessalonians*, rev. ed., The Daily Study Bible Series (Philadelphia, Pa.: Westminster Press, 1975), p. 70.

To these precious newborn Christians, Paul later writes,

> For who is our hope or joy or crown of exultation?
> Is it not even you, in the presence of our Lord Jesus
> at His coming? For you are our glory and joy.
> (1 Thess. 2:19–20)

Not only are these baby believers Paul's joy on earth, they will also be his crown of exultation "in the presence of our Lord Jesus at His coming." And so it will be for all believers who have taken part in the spiritual labor and delivery of newborn converts to Christ.

Who Qualifies as a Recipient of this "Crown"?

Commentator Joe L. Wall explains what it will be like for those who receive this crown:

> When we stand in the presence of Jesus at His royal coming, our hearts will overflow with pride, joy, and exultation because of those who stand with us at that time—those we have had a share in bringing to the Savior.
> What a thrill! For all eternity we will have "walking wreath-crowns" living and enjoying with us the glorious presence and unspeakable delights of life in the kingdom of the Prince of Peace.[2]

Imagine standing in heaven surrounded by all the people you have influenced for the sake of the gospel. Your dear sister or uncle or son. Your coworker or neighbor, the teenager you sat beside on the bus, or the many people who have come to Christ through the missionaries you've supported. What a thrill indeed!

This crown is for all of us who share the good news of salvation with the many people who ebb and flow through our lives. It is available to every believer, not just to the evangelists and preachers.

With this in mind, let's spend some time now strengthening our ability to witness, to effectively share Christ. This way we, too, can experience more of the joys of spiritual childbirth now and throughout eternity.

---

2. Joe L. Wall, *Going for the Gold* (Chicago, Ill.: Moody Press, 1991), p. 153.

Some Guidelines for Sharing Our Faith

To find our way along this path of joy, we will turn to the story of Philip in Acts 8 and draw out seven guidelines for sharing our faith. Philip, along with other believers, has been driven out of Jerusalem by the angry winds of persecution (v. 1). When he reaches the city of Samaria, God uses him powerfully, and people begin streaming in to trust Christ (vv. 5–8).

Waist-deep in this glorious success, Philip suddenly feels an unexpected tap on his shoulder:

> An angel of the Lord spoke to Philip saying, "Arise and go south to the road that descends from Jerusalem to Gaza." (This is a desert road.) (v. 26)

Obedience

Philip could have objected. "Leave Samaria? Now? Who will take my place? Things are rolling here—it's just beginning to get fun!" Instead, according to the next verse, "he arose and went" (v. 27a). His response illustrates the first guideline in sharing our faith: obedience. When God's children obey, doors open, blessings come, and lives are forever changed, because obedience always yields spiritual dividends. So, obediently following the Lord, Philip travels from the verdant pastureland of Samaria to the daunting desert of Gaza—just like Abraham, "not knowing where he was going" (Heb. 11:8b).

Availability

Coming to that hot, dusty road to Gaza, Philip must have thought, "Well, Lord, now what do I do? You must have some purpose for me here."

> And behold, there was an Ethiopian eunuch, a court official of Candace, queen of the Ethiopians, who was in charge of all her treasure; and he had come to Jerusalem to worship. And he was returning and sitting in his chariot, and was reading the prophet Isaiah. And the Spirit said to Philip, "Go up and join this chariot." (Acts 8:27b–29)

Philip's attitude reflects our second guideline: availability. Because he is open to the Holy Spirit's leading, he is able to perceive

God's reason for his unplanned desert trip—to cross paths with this searching Ethiopian.

A Proper Approach

Bringing the evangelist and the Ethiopian together, the Lord now leaves the next move up to Philip.

> When Philip had run up, he heard him reading Isaiah the prophet, and said, "Do you understand what you are reading?" (v. 30)

Philip wisely employs one of the most effective approaches in initiating a conversation about Christ: he asks a question.[3] Then he simply waits for the Ethiopian to answer him and open the door for a discussion about Christ.

Tactfulness

Obviously, the Holy Spirit has been preparing the Ethiopian for this "chance" meeting, because his answer gives Philip a perfect entrée to share the gospel message.

> And he said, "Well, how could I, unless someone guides me?" And he invited Philip to come up and sit with him. (v. 31)

Notice that Philip respectfully waited for the Ethiopian to invite him onto the chariot. He didn't automatically hop on board, kick off his sandals, and call the man "pal." Neither did he whip out his seminary degree and fill the man's ear with a twenty-minute exegesis of the passage. Instead, Philip was tactful. In fact, he mostly kept quiet at first because he wanted to understand the Ethiopian's particular needs.[4] By listening to him, Philip then knew exactly where to begin his presentation of the gospel.

---

3. Philip's question was ingenious. Whether the man said yes or no, that he did or did not understand the passage, Philip could have initiated a discussion with him.

4. When we share the gospel with people, discovering their needs is essential. For instance, a person may be the proud type or the religious type. He or she may be indifferent, antagonistic, angry, or suspicious. Some people have been disillusioned by religion in the past, and they need special care. Being interested in the other person demonstrates courtesy and tactfulness.

Begin Where the Person Is

Philip soon discovers what is confusing the eunuch.

> The passage of Scripture which he was reading was this:
>
>> "He was led as a sheep to slaughter;
>> And as a lamb before its shearer is silent,
>> So He does not open His mouth.
>> In humiliation His judgment was taken
>>   away;
>> Who shall relate His generation?
>> For His life is removed from the earth."
>
> And the eunuch answered Philip and said, "Please tell me, of whom does the prophet say this? Of himself, or of someone else?" (vv. 32–34)

This question provides Philip the starting point to explain that Christ is the subject of these prophecies—the promised Messiah who died for our sin. The Ethiopian was receptive to this truth because Philip didn't set him up or corner him. He simply listened and cared, and when the opportunity presented itself, he began where the eunuch was and then spoke boldly about Christ.

Focus on Jesus Christ

Philip could have tried to enliven his conversation by posing a few controversial questions. Or he could have complicated his presentation with the latest intellectual trumpery. He could have become argumentative or gotten sidetracked on a dozen rabbit trails. But instead, he stayed on the essential subject: Jesus Christ.

> Philip opened his mouth, and beginning from this Scripture he preached Jesus to him. (v. 35)

Philosophy has never saved anyone; only a relationship with God through the mediator Christ can produce the newborn cry of spiritual life in a person's heart. So Jesus must be our focus, for He is the One who has paid sin's debt and now offers us God's forgiveness, full and free. As this gospel message filled the Ethiopian's soul, he immediately responded, and Philip became the proud papa of a new baby believer.

Always Follow Up

The first sign of the eunuch's infant faith emerged quickly, for

> as they went along the road they came to some water; and the eunuch said, "Look! Water! What prevents me from being baptized?" And Philip said, "If you believe with all your heart, you may." And he answered and said, "I believe that Jesus Christ is the Son of God." And he ordered the chariot to stop; and they both went down into the water, Philip as well as the eunuch; and he baptized him. (vv. 36–38)

Philip was there to follow up the man's conversion with baptism. Likewise, it's important for us to stay involved with the newborn Christians we deliver into God's family. They need our nurturing in three areas. First, they need us to explain a few things, such as their security in the Lord and their salvation. Second, they need information: how to read the Bible, how to pray, how to confess sin. We might also recommend a good book on Christian basics or introduce them to an accountability group. Third, they need us to continue a relationship with them through phone calls, letters, or regular meetings. All this follow-up is like spiritual pediatrics—we're raising the new believer to be a strong, mature follower of Christ.

One Final Reminder

To witness for Christ, you don't have to stand on a street corner, blaring the gospel through a megaphone and stuffing tracts into people's pockets. The most effective soul winners are those who share Christ by their lifestyle. So let witnessing be natural; just be caring, tactful, and honest. You'll be amazed at how many opportunities you'll have to explain the gospel and experience the joy of spiritual childbirth.

 Living Insights STUDY ONE

How easy it is for a conversation about Christianity to devolve into an argument about politics or denominational differences or personal philosophy. What can we do to prevent our witnessing attempts from getting snagged on these thorny tangents? We can try to transition every side point back to the essential subject of Jesus Christ and the gospel.

Of course, in order to do this, we must first have a clear understanding of the gospel. The following outline, based on verses in Romans, is one of the clearest explanations:

- All have sinned (3:23).

- There is a penalty for sin (6:23).

- Christ suffered the penalty for our sin on the cross (5:8).

- We must trust Christ alone for salvation (10:9–10).

Take a moment to look up these verses and memorize this outline. Then, from the following typical statements made by unbelievers, practice developing transitions to bring the subject of the conversation back to the gospel. There are no right or wrong answers; this is just an opportunity for you to brainstorm ways to respond to these kinds of comments. As an example, we've filled out the first one for you.

- "In my opinion, we're all God's children, and as long as we do our best on earth, God will accept us into heaven."

  God does love us very much, like a father loves His children. But our sin has separated us from Him. In Romans 6:23, the Bible calls that separation "death" . . .

- "One denomination says this, another says that. Who knows what is right? I just follow God in my own way."

  _____

  _____

  _____

- "Those TV evangelists, all they want is money. I'd have to be pretty gullible to fall for their line."

  _____

_____

_____

_____

- "Religion is fine for people who need a crutch to lean on. I'm doing fine without it. Besides, church is just a haven for hypocrites."

_____

_____

_____

 Living Insights

Suppose you've explained the gospel to your unbelieving friends, but you sense that they are still reluctant to receive Christ. Why would they hesitate to accept such a wonderful gift? Here are a few possible reasons:

- They want to stay in their sinful condition.

- They are confused about what you've said.

- They're not really convinced the gospel is true.

- They are afraid.

- They feel too much pressure.

What can you do to show them respect and acceptance? Second Timothy 2:24–26 lays down some principles to follow in responding to those who don't agree with the gospel message. Take a moment to read these verses, then write down some ways you can apply the principles to a witnessing situation. We've given you a few examples.

"Not quarrelsome" — *I can allow plenty of room for questions.*

"Be kind" — *I can ask them if I've said something that offended them.*

"With gentleness" — *I can back off, letting them ponder the gospel on their own.*

_____

_____

_____

The devil will not easily give up your friends to the Lord. So be patient, love them consistently, pray for them often. This is your period of spiritual labor—maybe soon a new believer will be born.

Chapter 4

THE CROWNS OF
RIGHTEOUSNESS AND LIFE

2 Timothy 4:1–8; James 1:2–4, 12

Where is your heart? Not the muscle in your chest, but your inner self—what C. H. Spurgeon called "the mainspring of our motives."[1] Wound by visions of success and power, your heart may be in your career or investments. Set by longings for comfort and security, maybe your heart is in your house or your relationships. Wherever your dreams live, there you'll find your heart, for as Jesus said, "Where your treasure is, there will your heart be also" (Matt. 6:21).

One man whose heart was in the right place was Moses. Raised by Egyptian royalty, he ate the richest foods, enjoyed the grandest comforts, and studied under the finest teachers. Regal wealth dripped from his luxurious garments and glittering jewels. Surely Egypt's treasures tantalized Moses, yet he did not trade his heart for its pleasures. Rather,

> by faith Moses, when he had grown up, refused to be called the son of Pharaoh's daughter; choosing rather to endure ill-treatment with the people of God, than to enjoy the passing pleasures of sin; considering the reproach of Christ greater riches than the treasures of Egypt; for he was looking to the reward. (Heb. 11:24–26)

Where was Moses' heart? In his heavenly home, not his earthly palace. To him, the promise of God-given rewards outweighed all the treasures of Egypt, because God's crowns are celestial, not man-made; eternal, not fading away.

What Moses hoped for is also available to us when, like him, we consider the reproach of Christ greater riches than the treasures of this world. What was Moses' hope and reward? Because of his consistent obedience and willingness to endure trials, he has probably received at least these two: the crown of righteousness and the

---

1. Tom Carter, comp., *Spurgeon at His Best* (Grand Rapids, Mich.: Baker Book House, 1988), p. 94.

crown of life. Let's discover what the New Testament has to say about them.

The Crown of Righteousness

The apostle Paul refers to the crown of righteousness in his final epistle, 2 Timothy. Probing the context in which it appears will help us understand what it takes to win this crown.

The Context

When Paul penned 2 Timothy, death's shadow lengthened over him in his dark and lonely cell in Rome's Mamertine dungeon. He was a month, a day, maybe an hour away from standing before his Savior at the judgment seat. Probably the anticipation of that epochal moment prompted his urgent appeal to Timothy:

> I solemnly charge you in the presence of God and of Christ Jesus, who is to judge the living and the dead, and by His appearing and His kingdom: preach the word; be ready in season and out of season; reprove, rebuke, exhort, with great patience and instruction. (4:1–2)

"Preach the word," Paul exhorted. How? With persistence—"in season and out of season"—and with patience. Great patience. Why? Because change comes slowly, and for some, it may appear to not ever come at all. Also, though many would prefer to be entertained (vv. 3–4), what they really need is a steady diet of God's truth. Paul goes on to urge,

> Be sober in all things, endure hardship, do the work of an evangelist, fulfill your ministry. (v. 5)

In other words, "No matter what the hardship, Timothy, keep on preaching the Word." To borrow a popular slogan, Paul was telling him: "Just do it!"

The Confession

That against-all-odds determination has typified Paul's own ministry, but now his life is nearing its end. Confessing the inevitable, he says,

> I am already being poured out as a drink offering, and the time of my departure has come. (v. 6)

As he reflects on his years with Christ—his blinding-light conversion, his missionary travels, his painful sufferings—he has no regrets. Instead, leaving for Timothy a model that still challenges us today, he confidently writes,

> I have fought the good fight, I have finished the course, I have kept the faith. (v. 7)

The Greek word for *fight* is *agōn*, from which we derive our word *agony*. It was the term used for an athletic contest, such as a wrestling match. Throughout Paul's life, many opponents had challenged him, yet not once did he shrink away from a hand-to-hand battle for truth.

He also finished the course. He may have made mistakes along the way, stumbled, or felt like giving up, but still he ran hard, keeping his eyes on Christ, waiting at the finish line.[2]

And he ran the course unwaveringly. From that fateful day on the Damascus road to his present Roman imprisonment, he never compromised his integrity or his commitment to the Lord. What a legacy of perseverance!

The Crown

And now, like an athlete standing on the victor's platform, he excitedly anticipates receiving his crown.

> In the future there is laid up for me the crown of righteousness, which the Lord, the righteous Judge, will award to me on that day; and not only to me, but also to all who have loved His appearing. (v. 8)

This crown of righteousness is not his alone; it is for all of us who yearn for Christ's return. Woodrow Michael Kroll expands Paul's meaning.

> Those who realize they are but strangers and pilgrims here, and have set their affections on things above, will not be contented until the Lord comes again. . . . The crown of righteousness is awarded to all

---

2. The writer to the Hebrews describes how Paul ran his race and how we must run our races in order to finish well: "Therefore, since we have so great a cloud of witnesses surrounding us, let us also lay aside every encumbrance, and the sin which so easily entangles us, and let us run with endurance the race that is set before us, fixing our eyes on Jesus, the author and perfecter of faith" (Heb. 12:1–2a).

those who practice a life of righteousness and are constantly "Looking for that blessed hope, and the glorious appearing of the great God and our Saviour Jesus Christ" (Titus 2:13).[3]

What, then, does it take to win the crown of righteousness? According to Paul's example and instructions to Timothy, it takes:

- Fighting the good fight
- Finishing well
- Maintaining the faith
- Loving Christ's appearing through it all

The Crown of Life

What it takes to win the crown of life varies slightly from the requisites for winning the crown of righteousness. James describes the requirements for this next crown in his teaching about coping with trials.

Encountering Various Trials . . . Joy!

James addresses his epistle to "the twelve tribes who are dispersed abroad" (1:1b). These Jewish believers were

> being hunted under the persecution instigated by the Roman emperor Claudius. They had been hounded from their homes and homeland and were constantly being treated with hostility—by Gentiles, who hated them because they were Jewish, and by fellow Jews, who hated them for being Christians. These believers knew the bruised and bloodstained misery of troubles that wouldn't go away.[4]

So James encourages these battle-weary Christians to gain a new perspective on their circumstances.

---

3. Woodrow Michael Kroll, *It Will Be Worth It All* (Neptune, N.J.: Loizeaux Brothers, 1977), p. 98.

4. From the study guide *James: Practical and Authentic Living*, coauthored by Lee Hough, from the Bible-teaching ministry of Charles R. Swindoll (Fullerton, Calif.: Insight for Living, 1991), p. 17.

> Consider it all joy, my brethren, when you
> encounter various trials. (v. 2)

J. B. Phillips, in his *New Testament in Modern English*, translates the verse this way:

> When all kinds of trials and temptations crowd
> into your lives, my brothers, don't resent them as
> intruders, but welcome them as friends!

We usually consider them just the opposite, don't we? Why does James recommend we embrace them with joy? The answer lies not in the hardships themselves, but in how they deepen our character. As James says, "the testing of your faith produces endurance" (v. 3).

Enduring through Trials . . . Maturity!

The Greek word for *endurance*, *hupomenō*, literally means "to abide under." As the tests of faith rain down harder and harder, we develop more and more ability to abide under the pressure. As a result, hard times make us "perfect and complete, lacking in nothing" (v. 4b). In other words, they make us mature.

Maturity does not occur overnight. There are no get-mature-quick shortcuts. It takes time—only the Lord knows how much time it takes to accomplish His goals for us. But if we try to escape trials prematurely, we may short-circuit God's plan and forfeit the crown He has waiting for us.

Persevering under Trials . . . Crown!

James describes this crown in verse 12:

> Blessed is a man who perseveres under trial; for once
> he has been approved, he will receive the crown of life,
> which the Lord has promised to those who love Him.

What a ray of hope for those of us who have endured one storm swell after another! James calls us "blessed," or happy, beyond measure, because we have been approved—we have passed the test and persevered through the pain to glorify Christ in our suffering. Such unsinkable faithfulness will win us the crown of life.

May We Encourage You Today?

Right now, you may be enduring a hailstorm of trials that just won't go away. Based on what it takes to win the crowns of righteousness and life, here are two bits of advice that can help keep your eyes on the Lord and your heart in the right place.

First, *the roots grow deep when the winds are strong.* Like a cypress tree clinging to a cliff in a storm, we may think we'll blow away at any moment. But while the wind rages, the roots of our character are silently growing deep and strong. Knowing this helps us accept our hard times and see them as a necessary part of our personal development.

Second, *"there is no pit so deep that He is not deeper still."*[5] As she was dying, Betsie ten Boom whispered these words to her sister Corrie in the lice-infested Nazi concentration camp called Ravensbruck. These two women were experiencing a pit almost as deep and horrible as hell itself, yet even in that loathsome place, God was still there. In her book *The Hiding Place,* Corrie recalled a moment when she keenly felt His presence as Betsie read from her Bible to a group of women huddled in their barracks.

> Like waifs clustered around a blazing fire, we gathered about it, holding out our hearts to its warmth and light. The blacker the night around us grew, the brighter and truer and more beautiful burned the word of God. "Who shall separate us from the love of Christ? Shall tribulation, or distress, or persecution, or famine, or nakedness, or peril, or sword? . . . Nay, in all these things we are more than conquerors through him that loved us."
>
> I would look about us as Betsie read, watching the light leap from face to face. More than conquerors. . . . It was not a wish. It was a fact. We knew it, we experienced it minute by minute—poor, hated, hungry. We are more than conquerors. Not "we shall be." We are! Life in Ravensbruck took place on two separate levels, mutually impossible. One, the observable, external life, grew every day more horrible. The other, the life we lived with God, grew daily better, truth upon truth, glory upon glory.[6]

5. Betsie ten Boom, as quoted by Corrie ten Boom, with John and Elizabeth Sherrill, in *The Hiding Place* (New York, N.Y.: Bantam Books, 1971), p. 217.

6. Corrie ten Boom, *The Hiding Place*, pp. 194–95.

God will meet you in your pain, just as He met Corrie and Betsie in Ravensbruck. He is with you in the darkness, cultivating in you a more mature faith and preparing you to receive a conqueror's crown.

 ## Living Insights

The following questions are based on the requirements for winning the crown of righteousness. In your heart's inner room, make space for them and see what answers you discover.

- Am I fighting the good fight? Or am I dancing with my enemies: the world, the flesh, and the devil?

- Am I finishing the course? Or have I wandered into the grandstand, sipping lemonade and watching the athletes on the field?

- Am I maintaining my faith? Or has it fallen into disrepair, becoming rusty from lack of use?

- Am I hoping for Christ's return? Or have I asked Him to take a number and wait in line behind the other priorities in my life?

As you examine the following Scripture passages, allow the Holy Spirit to point out the areas in your life that fall short of what it takes to win the crown of righteousness. Write down what the Spirit is revealing and the crown-winning steps you can take.

- *Fighting the good fight*—Hebrews 3:6–15

_____

_____

_____

- *Finishing well*—Hebrews 12:1–2

_____

_____

_____

- *Maintaining the faith*—James 2:14–20

_____

_____

_____

- *Loving Christ's appearing*—Romans 8:22–25; 1 John 2:28–3:2

_____

_____

_____

When Paul looked back on his life, he could say with confidence, "I have fought the good fight, I have finished the course, I have kept the faith" (2 Tim. 4:7). May you be as confident when the sun sets on your earthly days and dawns on your heavenly eternity.

Living Insights

We are familiar with the trials of Job, how he lost his children, his health, and all he owned. You may recall what precipitated the tragedies—Satan's behind-the-scenes challenge to God:

> "Put forth Thy hand now and touch all that [Job] has;
> he will surely curse Thee to Thy face." (Job 1:11)

Philip Yancey, in his book *Disappointment with God*, calls this "The Wager . . . in which God 'risks' the future of the human experiment on a person's response."[7] But there is another wager in this story, equally precarious:

> The second wager, reflecting the human viewpoint, is the one that Job himself engaged in: should he choose for God or against him? Job weighed the evidence, most of which did not suggest a trustworthy

7. Philip Yancey, *Disappointment with God* (Grand Rapids, Mich.: Zondervan Publishing House, 1988), p. 252.

God. But he decided, kicking and screaming all the way, to place his faith in God.[8]

If you are enduring a severe trial right now, you may also be deciding whether to choose for God or against Him. This may not be an easy choice; for if the truth be known, you're mad at Him, and, frankly, it's hard to trust someone you're angry with.

Because life hurts so much, advice to "count it all joy" has an insensitive ring to it. Perhaps the best recommendation we can offer is the encouragement given by the writer to the Hebrews. Take a moment to read Hebrews 10:32–39.

Describe the Hebrew believers' trials and how they initially responded to them (vv. 32–34).

_____

_____

_____

In spite of their strong faith at first, the people were weakening. So the writer exhorts them, "Do not throw away your confidence" (v. 35a). What positive motivation does he offer them to stay faithful to the Lord (vv. 35b–36)?

_____

_____

What negative motivation (vv. 37–39)?

_____

_____

Like Job, who never knew about Satan's challenge, we may never understand all the reasons for our suffering. We do, however, know the outcome of our faith: the reward of heaven. So "do not throw away your confidence." Keep on trusting God and looking to Jesus—who is at the finish line, urging you on with the promise:

> "Be faithful until death, and I will give you the crown of life." (Rev. 2:10b)

---

8. Yancey, *Disappointment with God*, p. 252.

Chapter 5

THE UNFADING CROWN OF GLORY

1 Peter 5:1–4

Imagine having a week like this: On Monday, you awake to find a yellow rose on your nightstand and a note that reads, "You're the greatest!" On Tuesday, a friend smiles and says, "Thanks for caring." On Wednesday, your neighbor brings you a plate of warm chocolate chip cookies. On Thursday, you receive a handwritten thank-you note from your pastor for your volunteer work. On Friday, your spouse surprises you with an evening on the town "because you deserve it." On Saturday, you work hard to clean the house, and your family notices! Finally, on Sunday, your youngest child draws your portrait in crayon and writes "I love you, xxxxxooooo" across the bottom of the page.

What a week that would be! Though your load of responsibility would not have lightened, your drudgery would have turned into delight and your weariness into strength because you'd been affirmed and appreciated.

Being appreciated is what heavenly rewards are all about. Christ hasn't forgotten or ignored our labor for Him; and someday, He will tangibly show His appreciation to us with crowns.[1]

We have come in our study to the fifth and final crown described in Scripture. Before examining it, though, let's briefly review the other four crowns and what it takes to win them.

Where We Have Been

The *incorruptible crown* is awarded for self-control, being able to say "no" to the flesh. The *crown of exultation or joy* goes to those who care passionately for the lost and consistently share the gospel with them. For obeying Christ and anticipating His return, we will win the *crown of righteousness*. And for bringing glory to the Lord by enduring suffering with patience, we will receive the *crown of life*.

---

1. What will these crowns look like? We can't be sure that they are literal crowns of sparkling gold, fit perfectly to the size of our heads; the Bible may have used "crowns" simply as a metaphor to which we could relate. But one thing is certain—there will be actual, tangible rewards.

Christ Himself will distribute these crowns at the judgment seat, so we can be sure they will be given fairly and without partiality. No one will step in line ahead of us or elbow us out of receiving our rewards. They are safe in His hands, waiting for that thrilling moment when He grants them to us.

Then, after we have received them, we will glorify Jesus by giving Him our most precious possessions—our crowns. As one great body of believers, we will cast them at His feet; for truly, He is the only One worthy "to receive glory and honor and power" (Rev. 4:11).[2]

And Now . . . for Shepherds Only

The fifth crown, the unfading crown of glory, is unique because it is reserved for the *presbuteros*—the elders. These Christians were "the officials who acted as pastoral leaders of the congregations."[3] Today this group would include pastors as well as lay leaders in the church and other Christian ministries. These are the "shepherds" of the church, and the apostle Peter has specific instructions for them about what it takes to win this crown.

Context and Subject

He addresses the elders, not as their high-ranking pope, but as their

> fellow elder and witness of the sufferings of Christ,
> and a partaker also of the glory that is to be revealed.
> (1 Pet. 5:1)

As a "fellow elder," or *sumpresbuteros*, Peter is one of them. He understands the demands on their lives and feels the same pressures they feel. He is also a "witness," a *martus*, since he has seen the sufferings of Christ firsthand. And he is a "partaker"—partner— with them in the coming glory . . . the coming moment when they will all receive their rewards.

We could say that Peter is speaking to them as a player-coach.

---

2. Revelation 4:10 refers to the twenty-four elders casting their crowns before the throne of Christ. In John's vision, this group probably represents the universal church, including all Christians throughout time.

3. Fritz Rienecker, *A Linguistic Key to the Greek New Testament*, ed. Cleon L. Rogers, Jr. (Grand Rapids, Mich.: Zondervan Publishing House, Regency Reference Library, 1980), p. 765.

He plays on the team and knows their struggles, yet, at the same time, has some well-qualified words of counsel for them.

Command and Qualifications

Peter's opening instruction to his fellow *presbuteros* is rich with meaning and imagery: "Shepherd the flock of God among you" (v. 2a). The metaphor of a shepherd beautifully pictures the responsibilities of elders. Just as shepherds lead their sheep, so elders should lead the people in their care. They are to live among them and stay with them through seasons of sunshine or rain. They are to pay attention to them and pray for them. With rods of wisdom in their hands, elders should protect the people from ravenous false teachers. And when some of their flock stray from the Lord, they are to rescue them and gently guide them back to the right path.

We often think of elders as preachers or teachers or administrators. But primarily, they are shepherds, serving and loving God's flock. Notice, the flock is not their own; it is God's. He owns the sheep, and the shepherds merely care for those God has entrusted to them.

How elders care for God's flock is the subject Peter addresses next. The following chart diagrams his three contrasting statements.

Negative	Positive
Not under compulsion	*but* voluntarily
Not for sordid gain	*but* with eagerness
Not lording it over them	*but* proving to be an example

If we look at the first pair of contrasts, we find that being an elder is a calling from God, not a job where you punch the time clock. Something tragic happens when leaders lose their sense of calling, their ministry becomes militant, distant, a grinding duty instead of a joy. "One more year, and I'm done with my term," an elder might complain. "Meetings, meetings, meetings. How did I ever get coerced into this thankless job?"

Instead, they need to lead voluntarily and with enthusiasm— "according to the will of God." In Greek, this phrase is simply *kata theon*, "according to God"; "the will of" was added by the Bible translators to help us understand the phrase's meaning. If we take that added phrase out, though, we see that elders are to lead as God leads, willingly and sacrificially.

The second contrast, "not for sordid gain, but with eagerness," focuses on an elder's motive (2b). Greed can be a subtle invader, creeping into a pastor's heart so that receiving a paycheck or privileges is thought of more eagerly than serving Christ. Christian leaders can become like bellboys—doing God's work, then holding out their hand for a little something extra.

On the flip side, congregations should recompense their pastoral team well. Substandard salaries can force pastors to focus on money and rationalize their growing greed. So both the congregation and the leadership have a role in ensuring that money is not an issue for the shepherd of the flock.

Third, elders are to oversee the people, yet not

> as lording it over those allotted to your charge, but proving to be examples to the flock. (v. 3)

When shepherds start lording it over the flock, they stop leading and start manipulating. They model less and control more. They become unaccountable and arrogant—tyrants in their own little kingdoms. God's unfading crown of glory, however, cannot be won by ordering the flock around, expecting the sheep to jump at every command. Instead, shepherds are to "be examples."

Example in Greek is *tupos*, which can mean "an *impression, impress,* the *stamp* made by a die; hence, *a figure, image.*"[4]

In other words, a *tupos* is a model of the original. Who is the original for shepherds to pattern themselves after? The Chief Shepherd, Jesus Christ. During His life on earth, He displayed every characteristic needed by elders today—self-control, discernment, humility, gentleness, determination, and discipline. He was strong enough to confront a good friend with the terrible words, "Get behind Me, Satan" (Matt. 16:23a), sensitive enough to feel a sick woman's touch of faith in a crowd (Mark 5:25–34), and patient enough to endure intense suffering, surrendering Himself to the will of the Father.

And like Christ, Christian leaders, too, become the target of criticism. They will make mistakes, be misunderstood, and become weary. They may even yearn to fight back or document their defenses. But sometimes the best course of action a leader can take is to simply take it on the chin. Leave some notes unanswered. Leave the critics alone . . . and remember that Jesus also faced jeers and persecution (see 1 Pet. 2:21–23).

---

4. G. Abbott-Smith, *A Manual Greek Lexicon of the New Testament,* 3d ed. (Edinburgh, Scotland, T. and T. Clark, 1937), p. 452.

Promise

In the end, what will be waiting for faithful shepherds?

> And when the Chief Shepherd appears, you will
> receive the unfading crown of glory. (5:4)

When all the misunderstandings are past, all the criticisms are over, and all the mistakes you made are history, God's words of appreciation and His crown of glory will make the hard road of leadership worthwhile.

What Does It Take to Win?

Joe L. Wall, in his book *Going for the Gold*, tells of a story in the *Houston Post* about a boy with cerebral palsy who decided to enter a local mini-marathon. Timmy's mother did what she could to talk him out of it; after all, he had difficulty walking down the block, much less running several miles. Still, he was determined. On the day of the race, Timmy lined up beside the other participants, and with the bang of the starter's gun he was off.

> As the other racers took off at full stride, he began
> to move forward slowly, favoring his good left leg
> and nursing along his unsynchronized right leg as
> best he could.
>   Another man won the mini-marathon in 32
> minutes and 23 seconds. Timmy crossed the line in
> 2 hours and 6 minutes—dead last. But, as the head-
> line of the article so accurately recorded, that day
> "The Real Winner Came in Last."[5]

Timmy was a winner, not because he took first place, but because he had the determination to finish that race. Pastors, elders, and Christian leaders, it is not necessarily the amount of talent you have, it's your faithfulness to the task Christ has set before you that makes you a winner in His eyes. It's your volunteer spirit, your eager attitude, and your humble modeling of Christ that will win you the unfading crown of glory.

So get ready to run the race, not with your heart set on hearing human applause, but with your eyes fixed on the glory to come and the reward laid up for you in heaven.

5. Joe L. Wall, *Going for the Gold* (Chicago, Ill.: Moody Press, 1991), pp. 169–70.

Many pastors or Christian leaders don't feel appreciated. Months can go by without anyone stopping to say thanks or to give them a simple pat on the back. Just as God plans to honor our shepherds with the unfading crown of glory, we can also crown them with our appreciation for their hard work. From the following verses, write down how you can support your leaders in their ministries.

1 Corinthians 16:15–18 _____

_____

Philippians 2:25–29 _____

_____

1 Thessalonians 5:12–13 _____

_____

Hebrews 13:7, 17–18 _____

_____

With these Scriptures in mind, plan a few practical ways you can show your appreciation. To start your thinking, ask yourself, How would I want to be appreciated if I was in my leader's shoes? Don't delay in carrying out your plan; your shepherd has probably been longing for a cool drink of affirmation from someone just like you.

_____

_____

_____

_____

_____

_____

Living Insights

Section 1 of this study guide was a look at what it takes to win the heavenly crowns. Section 2 will examine in further detail our present-day objectives on the way to our eternal goals. Before embarking on that section, however, let's review the crowns one last time. The following exercise lists the crown, what it takes to win it, and space to write steps you can take now to achieve it.

Goal: The Imperishable Crown

Definition: Self-control, saying "no" to sin.

My steps: _____

_____

_____

_____

Goal: The Crown of Exultation

Definition: Sharing Christ and making disciples.

My steps: _____

_____

_____

_____

Goal: The Crown of Righteousness

Definition: Faithful obedience and living in light of Christ's appearing.

My steps: _____

_____

_____

_____

Goal: The Crown of Life

Definition: Enduring suffering so that Christ is glorified.

My steps: _____

_____

_____

_____

Goal: The Unfading Crown of Glory

Definition: Modeling Christ as a shepherd of God's flock.

My steps: _____

_____

_____

_____

OUR
PRESENT
OBJECTIVES

Chapter 6

DOING MINISTRY THE RIGHT WAY . . . FOR THE RIGHT REASONS

2 Corinthians 4:1–7

Ministries are like houses. On the outside, they may appear well-built and sturdy, but once you move in, it doesn't take long to discover the hidden flaws.

For a moment, stroll through the ministry with which you're involved, and put a few of its features to the test. When you turn on a faucet, does a clear stream of biblical truth flow out, or have some worldly contaminants polluted the water? Do the doors to the leaders' lives swing open freely, or are they stuck shut? When hard times rain down, does the roof provide protection, or do grumblings and complaints trickle down the walls and drip from the ceilings?

If your "house" needs remodeling, maybe the reason is that it was built using faulty construction methods. In this chapter, we'll study some essentials for building a ministry the right way—a way that may require us to leave behind our old familiar tools in favor of new ones that better communicate the gospel message.

A Primary Principle to Be Reviewed

Change is seldom easy, but it is often a necessary part of growth. Jesus capsulized this idea for us when He said,

> "No one puts a patch of unshrunk cloth on an old garment; for the patch pulls away from the garment, and a worse tear results. Nor do men put new wine into old wineskins; otherwise the wineskins burst, and the wine pours out, and the wineskins are ruined; but they put new wine into fresh wineskins, and both are preserved." (Matt. 9:16–17)

This chapter elaborates on the general topics introduced in chapter 5, "The Unfading Crown of Glory."

From this truth we can draw one primary principle of ministry: *We must be willing to leave the familiar methods without disturbing the essential message.* If we aren't willing to change, we risk having a cold, lifeless dust settle on our ministries as time moves by us.

Flexibility is essential, and the apostle Paul shows us three ways to build this into our ministries in 2 Corinthians 4:1–7. Let's follow the master craftsman verse by verse.

> Therefore, since we have this ministry, as we received mercy, we do not lose heart. (v. 1)

The first truth we can hammer in place is that *with every ministry, special mercy is needed.* God grants a special mercy for ministry in Brussels, which is different from the special mercy needed in Brooklyn, which is different from the special mercy for Bangkok. The way we minister differs with each culture, and God's special mercies enable us to keep at the task without losing heart.

Our second truth is found in verse 2:

> But we have renounced the things hidden because of shame, not walking in craftiness or adulterating the word of God, but by the manifestation of truth commending ourselves to every man's conscience in the sight of God.

From these words of Paul, we learn that *in every ministry, some things have to be renounced and rejected.* Notice the three "things" Paul referred to: (1) hiding shameful things, (2) doing deceitful things—"walking in craftiness," and (3) corrupting precious things—"adulterating the word of God."

By not renouncing these things and thus compromising God's building standards, even though we may go through the motions of ministry, we forfeit His blessing. This principle holds true for every ministry, large or small, urban or rural, local or foreign. It applies to parachurch or church ministries, denominational or nondenominational. Pastors may be green, fresh out of seminary, or ripe with experience; but if they and their churches hide sins, deceive one another, or corrupt the Scripture, that ministry will develop dry rot and eventually collapse from within.

Moving past verses 3 and 4, we can draw a third truth from verse 5:

> For we do not preach ourselves but Christ Jesus as Lord,

and ourselves as your bond-servants for Jesus' sake.

In other words, *through every ministry, a certain style must be modeled and communicated.* This style is preaching not "ourselves but Christ Jesus as Lord." We are to lift up His name, His person, His work, His message, His gospel, His presence, His power, His glory, His truth, His style, His approach, His thinking. And by lifting up Christ and removing ourselves from the spotlight, we model servanthood—becoming "bond-servants for Jesus' sake."

Sometimes, we try to share Christ's acclaim and receive some of the applause due Him, but His throne is not built for two. If we truly worship Him as Lord, then our place is in service to Him and to one another. According to Paul, that is the proper place for us to be, because Christ's gospel is the true source of life within us.

> For God, who said, "Light shall shine out of darkness," is the One who has shone in our hearts to give the light of the knowledge of the glory of God in the face of Christ.
> But we have this treasure in earthen vessels, that the surpassing greatness of the power may be of God and not from ourselves. (vv. 6–7)

As earthen vessels, our stay on earth is temporary and our bodies and minds are frail, yet Christ has chosen to indwell us with the power of His Word. *He* is the treasure people come to see, not us. When we realize this, we are on our way to building lasting ministries.

Three Temptations to Be Resisted

Constructing a ministry the right way is only half the challenge; doing it for the right reasons is just as important. Let's consider three of the most threatening temptations that might lure us into sin and undermine our efforts.

First: *The temptation to be self-sufficient and self-reliant.* The more we lean on our own ingenuity and talent, the less we depend on the Lord. In the end, we become independent merchandisers of the gospel rather than loyal servants of the King.

Second: *The temptation to be spectacular.* Jesus Himself faced this temptation, as Henri Nouwen recalls.

> The second temptation to which Jesus was exposed was precisely the temptation to do something

49

spectacular, something that could win him great applause. "Throw yourself from the parapet of the temple and let the angels catch you and carry you in their arms." But Jesus refused to be a stunt man. He did not come to prove himself. He did not come to walk on hot coals, swallow fire, or put his hand in the lion's mouth to demonstrate that he had something worthwhile to say. "Don't put the Lord your God to the test," he said.[1]

Like Jesus, we must also resist the temptation to spotlight ourselves or our ministries by producing religious circuses. The role of a servant is not meant to be a showy one . . . and besides, who needs loud speakers and strobe lights since the gospel is so riveting, even when it stands alone?

Third: *The temptation to be powerful and in control.* This snare is the most subtle of the three, for although leadership is necessary for ministry, it is easy for leaders to begin manipulating instead of leading. According to Nouwen, this is not the way of love, but of power.

What makes the temptation of power so seemingly irresistible? Maybe it is that power offers an easy substitute for the hard task of love. It seems easier to be God than to love God, easier to control people than to love people, easier to own life than to love life. Jesus asks, "Do you love me?" We ask, "Can we sit at your right hand and your left hand in your Kingdom?" (Matthew 20:21).[2]

Jesus' answer to this question is the same to us as to His disciples:

"Whoever wishes to become great among you shall be your servant, and whoever wishes to be first among you shall be your slave; just as the Son of Man did not come to be served, but to serve, and to give His life a ransom for many." (Matt. 20:26–28)

Servanthood was the essence of Jesus' ministry; we can't build a ministry on anything else.

---

1. Henri J. M. Nouwen, *In the Name of Jesus: Reflections on Christian Leadership* (New York, N.Y.: Crossroad Publishing Co., 1989), p. 38.

2. Nouwen, *In the Name of Jesus*, p. 59.

Eight "Cannots" to Be Remembered

To maintain a servant's heart and a right perspective toward ministry, we've compiled the following eight statements for leaders to remember. They all begin with "we cannot," because the more we observe the Lord's supernatural power, the more we realize what we can and cannot do.

- We cannot control everything.
- We cannot change or fix anyone.
- We cannot explain many things.
- We cannot meet everyone's expectations.
- We cannot dodge the tough questions, decisions, or tasks.
- We cannot concern ourselves with who gets the credit.
- We cannot cling to the past.
- We cannot do what we do either in the flesh or on our own.

These statements do not imply that leaders have no responsibilities; responsibilities are woven through the tapestry of these eight "cannots." But they do free us to be servants of the living God, able to admit and accept our own limitations and to trust completely in Christ to do what we cannot do.

Five Statements to Be Reinforced

OK, we've seen what we cannot do, so what can we do? The following positive statements outline five principles upon which to build a solid ministry.

Whatever we do, let's do more with others and less all alone. Ministry is not a solo flight for daring adventurers. It's a community of people supporting one another with each member contributing his or her special gift.

Whenever we do it, let's place the emphasis on quality not quantity. Emphasizing numbers in ministry is dangerous because it can confuse our purpose and discourage quality. Excellence must be our goal, not expansion.

Wherever we minister, let's do it the same as if we were doing it with those who know us best. For those who travel to minister, it helps to imagine your family or members of your home church in the congregation. Would they agree that what you're saying is accurate? Are you exaggerating points? Keeping them in mind while you're on the road will help you stay accountable.

Whoever may respond, let's keep a level head. A thriving ministry will have its critics and fans. Keeping a level head means not allowing either group to tip us to the extremes of depression or cockiness.

However long we minister, let's model a servant-hearted attitude and a grace-oriented style. These two qualities were the joist and beam upon which all of Christ's ministry rested. May they also be the foundational principles of our lives as we construct our ministries in His name.

Living Insights

If you are a leader in a church or parachurch organization, take a few moments to compare your ministry with Paul's building standards in 2 Corinthians 4:1–7.

• Are you experiencing God's special mercy in your ministry? Explain how you have seen His hand at work.

_____

_____

_____

• Are you renouncing and rejecting sinful attitudes in your ministry? Are there any hidden, shameful things you need to address? Any deceitful things? Any corrupting of the Scripture?

_____

_____

_____

• Are you elevating Jesus and modeling His leadership style of servanthood in your ministry? What are some ways you can be more of a servant?

_____

_____

_____

We commend your willingness to be a leader; our prayer is that more men and women like you will step forward to be shepherds of Christ's flock and that you will not tire of doing good.

Living Insights

Christian leaders are only human; they have strengths and limitations just like everyone else. In spite of this fact, many leaders live under a cloud of guilt because they can't do everything well. As a minister himself, Henri Nouwen knows this feeling well.

> You could say that many of us feel like failed tight-rope walkers who discovered that we did not have the power to draw thousands of people, that we could not make many conversions, that we did not have the talents to create beautiful liturgies, that we were not as popular with the youth, the young adults, or the elderly as we had hoped, and that we were not as able to respond to the needs of our people as we had expected. But most of us still feel that, ideally, we should have been able to do it all and do it successfully.[3]

Have you ever felt guilty for not being able to do it all? If so, perhaps your expectations need some adjusting. Maybe you need a fresh understanding of what you can and cannot do.

Let's take the eight negative and five positive statements from our lesson and transform them into a creed you can make your own (see next page). There's space at the bottom for your signature, if you agree with all the points. If not, change the wording and personalize it. Let this be your creed. Copy it, enlarge it, frame it, and refer to it often so that when perfectionism blows the clouds of guilt overhead, you can sweep them away with a fresh breeze of grace.

---

3. Nouwen, *In the Name of Jesus*, pp. 38–39.

THE CHRISTIAN LEADER'S MINISTRY CREED

I Cannot Do Many Things

I cannot control everything.

I cannot change or fix anyone.

I cannot explain many things.

I cannot meet everyone's expectations.

I cannot dodge the tough questions, decisions, or tasks.

I cannot concern myself with who gets the credit.

I cannot cling to the past.

I cannot do what I do either in the flesh or on my own.

In What I Can Do,
I Make These Promises before God

Whatever I do, I will do more with others and less all alone.

Whenever I do it, I will place the emphasis on quality, not quantity.

Wherever I go to minister, I will do it the same as if I were doing it with those who know me best.

Whoever may respond, I will keep a level head.

However long I minister, I will model a servant-hearted attitude and a grace-oriented style.

Signed: _____

Chapter 7

MAN'S DISEASE, GOD'S DIAGNOSIS, CHRIST'S REMEDY

Romans 5:6–11

O f God's marvelous grace, the psalmist wrote,

> I waited patiently for the Lord;
> And He inclined to me, and heard my cry.
> He brought me up out of the pit of destruction, out
> of the miry clay;
> And He set my feet upon a rock making my footsteps
> firm.
> And He put a new song in my mouth, a song of
> praise to our God;
> Many will see and fear,
> And will trust in the Lord.
> (Ps. 40:1–3)

Sunk in a pit of sin, we flounder helplessly until Christ draws us out and sets us on solid ground before God. This act of grace is so simple to describe, yet so mysterious. Who can explain all the divine intricacies of our salvation?

With Paul's words in Romans 5:6–11 as our guide, let's explore a few of these truths, beginning where God finds us—in the miry clay.

What Were We Like before Christ?

In Romans 1–3, Paul reveals the depth of our sinful predicament. In chapter 4, he contrasts our condition with God's requirement of righteousness, using Abraham as an example of faith. Now, in chapter 5, he will unite the two concepts—man's condition and God's solution—in a striking portrait of grace.

This chapter, as well as the next one, elaborates on the general topics introduced in chapter 2, "The Imperishable Crown."

"While We Were Still Helpless"

Romans 5:6 begins, "For while we were still helpless." The Greek word for *helpless, asthenēs,* means "without strength."[1] It pictures the kind of powerlessness that comes with paralysis, revealing that in a spiritual sense, we were powerless to get up from our bed of sin or even lift a hand to help ourselves.

To use another metaphor, it was as if we were strapped in an out-of-control airplane that was plummeting toward the earth. We could do nothing to change its course; we were helpless.

"While We Were Yet Sinners"

To make matters worse, Paul next says that "we were yet sinners" (v. 8b). We weren't just innocent victims on sin's disastrous ride; we were willful participants. Consequently, we are without excuse. Earlier in his letter, Paul made this fact clear:

> Since the creation of the world His invisible attributes, His eternal power and divine nature, have been clearly seen, being understood through what has been made, so that they are without excuse. For even though they knew God, they did not honor Him as God, or give thanks; but they became futile in their speculations, and their foolish heart was darkened. (1:20–21)

Although God shone His light on us, we turned our back on it, choosing darkness instead. Which means that we not only sinned, we became sinners or "sinning ones"—*hamartōlos* in Greek. This word is derived from the verb, "to miss the mark."[2] We could imagine a novice archer, drawing back an arrow and letting it fly, only to miss the target entirely. Morally, we were like that archer, always missing the target of God's righteousness.

In fact, we didn't just miss, we fell "short of the glory of God" (3:23b). It was as if we were trying to jump from a pier in California all the way to Hawaii. Some of us may have jumped farther than others, but no one made it there. In that same sense, we may have tried to be good, but none of us were good enough. None of us met

---

1. G. Abbott-Smith, *A Manual Greek Lexicon of the New Testament,* 3d ed. (Edinburgh, Scotland: T. and T. Clark, 1937), p. 64.

2. Abbott-Smith, *Lexicon,* p. 23.

God's standard of perfection, because we were sinners.

"While We Were Enemies"

But that's not all. Paul intensifies his description of our Christ-less condition with one final word: *enemies*. Beyond helplessness, beyond falling short as sinners, Paul writes that "we were enemies" (5:10a).

The Greek word for *enemies* conveys active aggression: "hating, hostile."[3] "The mind set on the flesh is hostile toward God," writes Paul, using the same root word (8:7a). Before trusting Christ, we all were that way. If God tried to steer us one direction, we chose the other. As Isaiah pointedly summed up our stubborn nature: "Each of us has turned to his own way" (53:6).

Paul's three-word portrait of human nature reveals man's condition in its starkest form, comprising the doctrine theologians term "total depravity." Charles Ryrie helps us understand this doctrine more completely:

> Total depravity does not mean that everyone is as thoroughly depraved in his actions as he could possibly be, nor that everyone will indulge in every form of sin, nor that a person cannot appreciate and even do acts of goodness; but it does mean that the corruption of sin extends to all men and to all parts of all men so that there is nothing within the natural man that can give him merit in God's sight.[4]

Put simply, depravity does not mean that without Christ we are as *bad* as we could possibly be; rather, we are as *bad off* as we could possibly be. We are all passengers on the same sinking ship, and although some of us may rank morally higher than others, the ship is still going down. We don't need to be quibbling about who is better than whom; we need to be rescued!

How Did God Respond to Us?

The Lord responded to our desperate situation in four ways.

---

3. Abbott-Smith, *Lexicon*, p. 192.

4. Charles Caldwell Ryrie, *A Survey of Bible Doctrine* (Chicago, Ill.: Moody Press, 1972), p. 111.

He Loved Us

His first response was love.

> But God demonstrates His own love toward us, in
> that while we were yet sinners, Christ died for us.
> (Rom. 5:8)

We were sinners—His enemies—yet Christ gave up His life
for us. We have trouble understanding this, for

> one will hardly die for a righteous man; though per-
> haps for the good man someone would dare even to
> die. (v. 7)

Who would die for someone who was wicked? No one . . .
but Christ.

His sacrifice amazes us, because we are used to earning love. We
think that the better we perform, the more favor we merit. Not so
in God's rule book; His love is free. But we say, "Wasn't there
somebody a little deserving of His love?" Not one person.

So, with hearts as cold and prickly as ours, we wonder: Why
did He love us? The answer is in Moses' words to the Hebrew people.

> "The Lord did not set His love on you nor choose
> you because you were more in number than any of
> the peoples, for you were the fewest of all peoples,
> but because the Lord loved you." (Deut. 7:7–8a)

He loved us . . . because He loved us. It's as simple as that.

He Justified Us

In Romans 5:9a, Paul describes God's second response to our
miry state: "Much more then, having now been justified by His
blood." What exactly does *justified* mean?

> It does not simply mean "just as if I'd never sinned."
> That doesn't go far enough! Neither does it mean
> that God makes me righteous so that I never sin
> again. It means to be "declared righteous." Justifica-
> tion is God's merciful act, whereby He declares righ-
> teous the believing sinner while he is still in his
> sinning state. He sees us in our need, wallowing
> around in the swamp of our sin. He sees us looking
> to Jesus Christ and trusting Him completely by faith,

to cleanse us from our sin. And though we come to Him with all of our needs and in all of our darkness, God says to us, "Declared righteous! Forgiven! Pardoned!"[5]

Having declared us righteous, God accepts us in Christ and responds to us in a third way.

He Saved Us from Wrath

We shall be saved from the wrath of God through Him. (v. 9b)

God's dark cloud of judgment no longer overshadows us because He has saved us from wrath both now and in the future. Prior to trusting Christ, we lived each day not knowing whether God's sword would fall; but now we do not fear His punishment, for Christ has already endured it on our behalf.

He Reconciled Us

God's fourth response is climactic. Removing all the barriers between us and Himself, He embraces us—His former enemies.

For if while we were enemies, we were reconciled to God through the death of His Son, much more, having been reconciled, we shall be saved by His life. (v. 10)

When we trusted Christ, God reconciled us to Himself. That means He changed our relationship with Him so that we were no longer considered hostile opponents but beloved children. All offenses were remembered no more, the chasm of sin was bridged, and we could come home.

Why Did God Do That?

Woven into these verses is the reason God could offer us so much for nothing in return:

At the right time Christ died for the ungodly. . . .
While we were yet sinners, Christ died for us. . . .

5. Charles R. Swindoll, *Growing Deep in the Christian Life* (Portland, Oreg.: Multnomah Press, 1986), p. 238.

We were reconciled to God through the death of
His Son. (vv. 6b, 8b, 10b)

Christ's death opened the gate, and in flooded God's benefits—
His love, justification, salvation, and reconciliation. For through
the cross, the righteousness God required from us Christ provided;
the punishment God demanded for our sin Christ endured; and the
life God longed to give us Christ now offers.

If you still live in the miry clay of sin . . . won't you accept
Christ's offer of deliverance? No amount of good works can draw
you up from the pit; only Christ can lift you out and set you on
the rock of a right standing before God. Believe in Him today.

If He has already drawn you out . . . remember your moment
of salvation, and praise the Lord for His gracious response to your
dire situation. Put yourself in the place of Christian, John Bunyan's
protagonist in *The Pilgrim's Progress,* when at the Cross he first felt
the release of sin's burden from his back, and sing with him in his
joy:

> Thus far I did come laden with my sin;
> Nor could aught ease the grief that I was in,
> Till I came hither: what a place is this!
> Must here be the beginning of my bliss?
> Must here the burden fall from off my back?
> Must here the strings that bound it to me crack?
> Blessed cross! blessed sepulchre! blessed rather be
> The Man that there was put to shame for me![6]

Living Insights   STUDY ONE

This study constructs a solid doctrinal foundation for
accomplishing what it takes to win the imperishable crown.
Remember the requirements for that crown? Running the race to
win, maintaining self-control, and consistently saying "no" to sin.
This is only possible when we fully understand our position in
Christ. Because of what He has done for us on the cross, we can
win our daily battles with sin.

---

6. John Bunyan, *The Pilgrim's Progress* (Old Tappan, N.J.: Fleming H. Revell Co., 1903), p. 30.

Romans 6 helps us understand how. What does Paul mean when he says, "We have died with Christ" (v. 8, see also verses 5–6)?

_____

_____

The fact of Christ's resurrection from the dead brings Paul to what conclusions in verse 9?

_____

_____

God justifies us or declares us righteous because we are united with Christ in His death and resurrection. Read verses 11–13, and write down Paul's commands related to our daily walk that also depend on our union with Christ.

_____

_____

_____

_____

The two key verbs are "consider" and "present"; one has to do with our mind-set and the other with our actions. In what ways can you battle sin in your life using these two strategies?

_____

_____

_____

_____

Living Insights   STUDY TWO

William Barclay retells a story from the life of T. E. Lawrence, the famous "Lawrence of Arabia," that illustrates the extent of our Savior's love for us.

In 1915 he was journeying across the desert with

some Arabs. Things were desperate. Food was almost done, and water was at its last drop. Their hoods were over their heads to shelter them from the wind which was like a flame and full of the stinging sand of the sandstorm. Suddenly someone said, "Where is Jasmin?" Another said, "Who is Jasmin?" A third answered, "That yellow-faced man from Maan. He killed a Turkish tax-collector and fled to the desert." The first said, "Look, Jasmin's camel has no rider. His rifle is strapped to the saddle, but Jasmin is not there." A second said, "Someone has shot him on the march." A third said, "He is not strong in the head, perhaps he is lost in a mirage; he is not strong in the body, perhaps he has fainted and fallen off his camel." Then the first said, "What does it matter? Jasmin was not worth ten pence." And the Arabs hunched themselves up on their camels and rode on. But Lawrence turned and rode back the way he had come. Alone, in the blazing heat, at the risk of his life, he went back. After an hour and a half's ride he saw something against the sand. It was Jasmin, blind and mad with heat and thirst, being murdered by the desert. Lawrence lifted him up on his camel, gave him some of the last drops of precious water, slowly plodded back to his company. When he came up to them, the Arabs looked in amazement. "Here is Jasmin," they said, "Jasmin, not worth ten pence, saved at his own risk by Lawrence, our lord."[7]

Around some people, you may feel worthless. Even in your own eyes you may question your value. But to Christ, you are worth risking His own life to search for you, dying alone in the desert. Live today, secure in your value and overwhelmed by His love.

7. Rita Snowdon, as told by William Barclay in *The Letter to the Romans*, rev. ed., The Daily Study Bible Series (Philadelphia, Pa.: Westminster Press, 1975), p. 76.

Chapter 8

THE IMPORTANCE OF JUDGING OURSELVES
1 Corinthians 11:27–32

"The life which is unexamined is not worth living,"[1] Plato once said. When was the last time you looked deeply into the well of your soul? Perhaps it was in the early morning hours on a camping trip, when you sat beside a lake and watched the rising sun dance across the water. Maybe at sunset, when you stopped your car along a lonely road to view the play of colors in the sky. Or possibly when you stood beneath a canopy of stars on a warm summer night.

How precious are the times of introspection . . . yet, unfortunately, how rare. Why? In many ways, our modern society has programmed us to avoid quiet self-examination. "We live in a noisy, busy world," observes Jean Fleming in her book *Finding Focus in a Whirlwind World*.

> Silence and solitude are not twentieth-century words. They fit the era of Victorian lace, high-button shoes, and kerosene lamps better than our age of television, video arcades, and joggers wired with earphones. We have become a people with an aversion to quiet and an uneasiness with being alone.[2]

So, since it doesn't come naturally, we must learn to invite silence and solitude for regular visits. Because, according to Scripture, they are the Lord's emissaries, bringing us valuable opportunities for self-evaluation and growth.

The Scriptural Basis for Looking Within

The Bible portrays introspection as a cooperative effort between God and ourselves—we do the work together. Let's first examine what He does in our hearts when we open the sanctuary of our souls.

---

1. Plato, as quoted in *Bartlett's Familiar Quotations*, 15th ed., rev. and enl., ed. Emily Morison Beck (Boston, Mass.: Little, Brown and Co., 1980), p. 83.

2. Jean Fleming, *Finding Focus in a Whirlwind World*, as quoted by Donald S. Whitney in *Spiritual Disciplines for the Christian Life* (Colorado Springs, Colo.: NavPress, 1991), p. 176.

The Lord's Part

David provides us with an initial description of the Lord's part in this prayer:

> Examine me, O Lord, and try me;
> Test my mind and my heart.
> (Ps. 26:2)

As only He can, the Lord peers inside us and reveals our deepest thoughts and motives, one by one. Are they authentic? Are they pure? He comes not to condemn but to turn us away from harmful paths and into the path of life, as David echoes in Psalm 139:

> Search me, O God, and know my heart;
> Try me and know my anxious thoughts;
> And see if there be any hurtful way in me,
> And lead me in the everlasting way. (vv. 23–24)

David knew he needed God to rummage through his dark closets and throw light in the dark corners of his life; otherwise he would never see his own hurtful ways.

How we, too, need the Lord's loving scrutiny! Without His watchful care, we would be like pilots in a fog with only our faulty instincts to guide us. But when God illumines our hearts, we suddenly perceive what we must do and where we must go. The haze clears, and we see His face. And He guides us toward the light of His "everlasting way."

The writer to the Hebrews presents this truth in different terms, in a context of God-given rest:

> There remains therefore a Sabbath rest for the people of God. For the one who has entered His rest has himself also rested from his works, as God did from His. Let us therefore be diligent to enter that rest. (Heb. 4:9–11a)

Apart from God's scrutiny and guidance, we anxiously wander in circles—always working, always in a panic, never at rest. But when we diligently open ourselves to our omniscient Lord, the only One who is qualified to judge us, we can discover any sinful areas or disobedient, willful streaks that would keep us from God's gift of rest. And isn't it comforting to realize that nothing can escape His notice?

There is no creature hidden from His sight but all

things are open and laid bare to the eyes of Him with whom we have to do. (v. 13)

We may forget or overlook things that are harmful to us, but God will not. So we can relax in His grace, having confessed and been cleansed from our sins and restored to His path of righteousness.

This divine analysis does not occur automatically, however. In order for God to do His work in our hearts, we must "be diligent" in attending to our part in the process.

Our Part

With a vivid metaphor, Proverbs 20:27 describes our part in the cooperative effort of introspection:

> The spirit of man is the lamp of the Lord,
> Searching all the innermost parts of his being.

Matthew Henry illumines the meaning of this verse for us.

> The great soul of man is a divine light; it is the *candle of the Lord*, a candle of his lighting. Conscience, that noble faculty, is God's deputy in the soul; it is a candle not only lighted by him, but lighted for him. By the help of conscience we come to know ourselves. The spirit of a man has a self-consciousness (1 Cor. 2:11); it searches into the dispositions and affections of the soul, praises what is good, condemns what is otherwise.[3]

Like an explorer in the deep caverns of a quiet cave, the Holy Spirit takes us on a journey through our inner being, showing us who we are and how we are by the light of our own spirits. He searches all the chambers with us, room by room. Such a thorough investigation takes time, for He does not hurry through hearts.

Sadly, in our frantic world, how little time we have for quiet contemplation. We're so busy that we can't even stop to get to know ourselves. Yet all the while, the Spirit of God longs to take the lamp of our spirits and cast light on our feelings, thoughts, pains, and limitations. Although we may wish someone else could go

---

3. Matthew Henry, *Commentary on the Whole Bible* (Grand Rapids, Mich.: Zondervan Publishing House, Regency Reference Library, 1961), p. 770.

through this process for us, only we can sound the depths of our own souls. Even our parents or spouses can't fully know what's inside us. "For who among men," Paul asks rhetorically,

> knows the thoughts of a man except the spirit of the man, which is in him? (1 Cor. 2:11a)

But to those who love God, He has given an added advantage—the ability to perceive the hidden things:

> "Things which eye has not seen and ear has not
>   heard,
> And which have not entered the heart of man,
> All that God has prepared for those who love Him."
> (v. 9)

All of this is possible when we allow the Lord to patiently guide us to the truth about ourselves. Paul makes clear the importance of this divine disclosure later in 1 Corinthians, when he addresses the subject of the Lord's Table.

Looking Within through the Window of Communion

Paul received his instructions about communion from the Lord Himself, probably through a special revelation (11:23a). Christ instituted this practice so that we would remember His sacrificial death, according to Paul's recounting of the Last Supper:

> The Lord Jesus in the night in which He was betrayed took bread; and when He had given thanks, He broke it, and said, "This is My body, which is for you; do this in remembrance of Me." In the same way He took the cup also, after supper, saying, "This cup is the new covenant in My blood; do this, as often as you drink it, in remembrance of Me." For as often as you eat this bread and drink the cup, you proclaim the Lord's death until He comes. (vv. 23b–26)

As we partake of the elements, the bread and the cup, we proclaim in an unspoken sermon Christ's death. In this way, the Lord's Table is an object lesson of faith that has lasted through the centuries and will continue until Jesus comes again.

It is a time not only for remembrance and proclamation but also for intimate fellowship with Him, hence the name communion.

But this communing with Him must not be entered into unworthily, because

> whoever eats the bread or drinks the cup of the Lord
> in an unworthy manner, shall be guilty of the body
> and the blood of the Lord. (v. 27)

Certainly, in one sense, we are all unworthy, for none of us are without sin. However, according to theologian Charles Hodge, Paul's focus is the manner in which we observe communion:

> To eat or drink *unworthily* is in general to come to
> the Lord's table in a careless, irreverent spirit, with-
> out the intention or desire to commemorate the
> death of Christ as the sacrifice for our sins.[4]

The Corinthian believers were particularly careless and irreverent around the Lord's Table. Combining a church supper event with communion, these Christians were making a mockery of it by allowing wealthier members to gorge themselves and leaving poorer members to go hungry. Some even swilled the wine until they were drunk (vv. 20–21). Because of this raucousness, Paul warned them they "shall be guilty of the body and the blood of the Lord." Hodge explains this phrase:

> The man who tramples on the flag of his country,
> insults his country; and he who treats with indignity
> the representative of a sovereign, thereby offends
> the sovereign himself. In like manner, he who treats
> the symbols of Christ's body and blood irreverently
> is guilty of irreverence towards Christ.[5]

The proper way to participate in communion begins with self-examination—the kind of God-with-us introspection we looked at earlier. As Paul told the Corinthians:

> But let a man examine himself, and so let him eat
> of the bread and drink of the cup. (v. 28)

Paul's word for *examine, dokimazō* means "to approve after

---

4. Charles Hodge, *An Exposition of the First Epistle to the Corinthians* (reprint; Grand Rapids, Mich.: William B. Eerdmans Publishing Co., 1980), p. 231.

5. Hodge, *Epistle to the Corinthians*, p. 230.

examination."[6] Approval was Paul's goal, not dismissal. He was not trying to push people away from the Table; he was trying to draw them in. In essence, he was telling them, "Let the Lord light the lamp of your spirit and probe those recesses of your heart so that you can eat and drink worthily."

For those who refuse to take their inner life seriously, Paul gave a warning:

> He who eats and drinks, eats and drinks judgment
> to himself, if he does not judge the body rightly. For
> this reason many among you are weak and sick, and
> a number sleep. (vv. 29–30)

So severe were the Corinthian believers' abuses of the Lord's Table that God was disciplining some of them with weakness, sickness, and even death. Actually, their irreverence was only one sip of sin out of a cupful of churchwide degradations: jealousy, cliques, sexual immorality, court battles between believers, wild living, and chaotic worship. That's why Paul urgently pleaded with them to examine their lives closely, before it was too late.

An Examined Life Is Worth Living

"If we judged ourselves rightly," Paul added, "we should not be judged" (v. 31). Including himself in his counsel, he was saying, "If we kept short accounts with God, we'd never suffer His discipline." When He does judge us, though, we can be assured that

> we are disciplined by the Lord in order that we may
> not be condemned along with the world. (v. 32)

God may discipline us, but He doesn't put us in the same category as condemned unbelievers. In this life, we may feel the sting of a woodshed experience, but we'll never taste the cup of eternal damnation.

Embedded in Paul's instructions here is a twist on Plato's words: "The examined life *is* worth living." As you read this prayer of David, let it lend a voice to your own desire to invite God into the hidden recesses of your heart and make yours a life worth living.

---

6. Fritz Rienecker, *A Linguistic Key to the Greek New Testament*, ed. Cleon L. Rogers, Jr. (Grand Rapids, Mich.: Zondervan Publishing House, Regency Reference Library, 1980), p. 427.

Who can discern his errors? Acquit me of hidden
     faults.
Also keep back Thy servant from presumptuous
     sins;
Let them not rule over me;
Then I shall be blameless,
And I shall be acquitted of great transgression.
Let the words of my mouth and the meditation of
     my heart
Be acceptable in Thy sight,
O Lord, my rock and my Redeemer.
(Ps. 19:12–14)

Living Insights

Our perceptions of the Lord's Supper vary depending on our
church background. To broaden our understanding of this
multifaceted sacrament, let's take a look at some of its names and
related meanings with Frederick Buechner's help.

> [The] reenactment of the Last Supper is some-
> times called the *Eucharist* from a Greek word mean-
> ing thanksgiving, i.e., at the Last Supper itself Christ
> gave thanks, and on their part Christians have noth-
> ing for which to be more thankful.
>
> It is also called the *Mass* from *missa*, the word
> of dismissal used at the end of the Latin service. It
> is the end. It is over. All those long prayers and
> aching knees. Now back into the fresh air. Back
> home. Sunday dinner. Now life can begin again.
> *Exactly.*
>
> It is also called Holy Communion because when
> feeding at this implausible table, Christians believe
> that they are communing with the Holy One him-
> self, his spirit enlivening their spirits, heating the
> blood and gladdening the heart just the way wine,
> as spirits, can.
>
> They are also, of course, communing with each
> other. To eat any meal together is to meet at the
> level of our most basic need. . . .

To eat this particular meal together is to meet at the level of our most basic humanness, which involves our need not just for food but for each other. I need you to help fill my emptiness just as you need me to help fill yours.[7]

The next time your church celebrates the Lord's Supper, focus your thoughts on these four aspects. To prepare yourself further, look up the following related verses, noting in the space provided the truths you can meditate on as you partake of the Lord's Supper.

- Thanksgiving: Colossians 1:12–20 _____

_____

- New beginnings: 2 Corinthians 5:17 _____

_____

- Communing with the Lord: John 6:48–58 _____

_____

- Fellowshipping with each other: Hebrews 10:19–25 _____

_____

 Living Insights STUDY TWO

Does Jesus understand how busy our lives are and how bedraggled we feel sometimes? He didn't have to punch a time clock in the morning or make evening sales calls. He didn't have to take the kids to Little League and dance lessons and birthday parties between fixing meals, cleaning house, and holding down a second job. Compared to our hectic pace, His strolling through the countryside seems sedate. Or was it?

Take a moment to read Luke 5:12–16. What was pressuring Jesus and how did He respond to it?

_____

7. Frederick Buechner, *Wishful Thinking: A Theological ABC* (New York, N.Y.: Harper and Row, Publishers, 1973), pp. 52–53.

We can imagine Jesus tiptoeing away in the predawn hours to escape the pressing crowd. Was He being irresponsible to take time for silence and solitude? No. Yet often we think if we take ten minutes alone, the business will fail, the kids will burn down the house, and the spinning earth will suddenly grind to a stop.

The truth is, regular quiet times will energize our spirits and help us cope better with life's demands. In addition to the psalms we studied in the lesson, think over the benefits of silent self-examination, prayer, and meditation found in these passages from Psalms.

4:4–5 _____

46:10 _____

62:5–8 _____

63:6–8 _____

143:5–6 _____

When is the best time for you to be quiet before God? Where can you go to find solitude? Susanna Wesley, mother of the founders of Methodism, John and Charles Wesley, had a large family to care for and found it difficult to be alone during her day. Donald S. Whitney explains how she creatively solved the problem:

> It is well known that when she needed silence and solitude she would bring her apron up over her head and read her Bible and pray underneath it. Obviously that did not block out all noise, but it was a sign to her children that for those minutes she was not to be bothered and the older ones were to care for the younger.[8]

Whether you have to sneak away or hide under an apron, whatever it takes, find time for daily self-examination and reflection.

8. Whitney, *Spiritual Disciplines*, pp. 189–90.

Chapter 9

MY COMMITMENT TO CHRIST'S COMMISSION

Matthew 28:16–20; Mark 16:14–16; Acts 1:6–8

The phone rings.

"Hello?"

"Hi, this is Bill Jacobs."

"Bill! My youth pastor! Goodness, it's been years. How are you doing?"

"Just fine. Listen, I'm in town for a day or so; how about getting together at the old diner on the corner of Grand and Main? Are you free today?"

———◆———

For a little while, may we step into the shoes of your old friend and sit across from you at that diner? Let's settle into a window booth and just chat through the curling steam from our coffee. How's your family? Your job? What's been on your heart lately? As the conversation winds through updates and remembrances, it finally comes to rest on spiritual matters. Just as your mentor would do, we'd like to challenge you with a probing question. Don't answer right away. Think about it for a moment as you search your heart. Here it is: How is your commitment to Christ's commission? Is it still as active and alive as it used to be?

The commission we're referring to is found in Jesus' last instructions to His disciples, which we sometimes call the Great Commission:

> "Go therefore and make disciples of all the nations,
> baptizing them in the name of the Father and the
> Son and the Holy Spirit, teaching them to observe all
> that I commanded you; and lo, I am with you always,
> even to the end of the age." (Matt. 28:19–20)

Your response to our question may reveal one of four common

This chapter, as well as the next one, elaborates on the general topics introduced in chapter 3, "The Crown of Exultation."

attitudes concerning Christ's final command. For a moment, warm your hands on the coffee cup, and see if any of these attitudes describe you.

Four Common Attitudes regarding the Great Commission

The first attitude is reflected in the response, "It's not my job." It's an attitude of *specialization*, which betrays a belief that evangelism and missions are done only by a specially trained and gifted few. This is understandable; after all, we live in the day of the specialist. We have medical specialists, legal specialists, financial specialists, even plumbing specialists. Shouldn't something as important as the Great Commission be left to spiritual specialists? According to Joe Aldrich, in his book *Life-Style Evangelism*, that is the way a lot of us operate.

> For many, evangelism is what the pastor does on Sunday morning as he throws the lure over the pulpit, hoping some "fish" in the stained-glass aquarium will bite. The "layman's" job is simply to herd fish within the reach of the "big fisherman." . . .
>
> Many assume that evangelism is what Billy Graham does and thus remove themselves from involvement because they "don't have his gifts."[1]

But the Great Commission is for every Christian, not just the silver-tongued few. It is *our* job.

The second attitude expresses itself in the question, "Am I my brother's keeper?" Let's label this attitude *isolationism*, because when we respond this way we are often trying to hide from the world and its problems. The masses of people in Asia or Europe or the Middle East who need to hear the gospel overwhelm us. "What can we do? We are so few. Besides, what about the people here at home. We can't even help them!" So we distance ourselves from them to maintain our psychological equilibrium.

Another common attitude is *procrastination*. "We're just too involved in other things," we wayworn Christians lament. The job is a hassle and the kids are sick, money is tight and the calendar is packed. "Maybe someday," we say, "when things lighten up a little."

1. Joseph C. Aldrich, *Life-Style Evangelism* (Portland, Oreg.: Multnomah Press, 1981), pp. 17–18.

But life seldom gets less busy, and "someday" just never comes. We may sincerely wish to be more involved, but we never seem to have the time.

The fourth attitude is wrapped in a snug blanket of theology: "Christ is sovereign, isn't He? He found me, so He can find others without my help." This reflects *rejection* or *indifference*. Lifting the theological covers, we usually see two types of believers hiding underneath, one quite different from the other.

The first type John Stott calls the "rabbit-hole Christian." This is the kind of person who

> pops his head out of the hole, leaves his Christian roommate in the morning, and scurries to class, only to frantically search for a Christian to sit next to. . . . Thus he proceeds from class to class. When dinner time comes, he sits with all the Christians in his dorm at one huge table and thinks, "What a witness!" From there he goes to his all-Christian Bible Study, and he might even catch a prayer meeting where the Christians pray for the nonbelievers on his floor. (But what luck that he was able to live on the floor with seventeen Christians!) Then at night he scurries back to his Christian roommate. Safe! He made it through the day and his only contacts with the world were those mad, brave dashes to and from Christian activities.[2]

While these believers run from the world, a second group runs with the world, mirroring both society's sophistication and skepticism. With nose turned up to most evangelism techniques, they consider witnessing to be rather gauche and criticize those who try to share their faith. "Before we criticize . . ." Leighton Ford reminds us,

> we ought to remember Moody's classic reply to a critic who disapproved of his methods. "I don't like them too much, myself," he admitted—"what method do you use?" When the critic said that he used none, Moody tartly replied, "Well, I think I

---

2. John Stott, as quoted by Rebecca Pippert in *Pizza Parlor Evangelism* (Downers Grove, Ill.: InterVarsity Press, 1976), p. 20, as quoted by Aldrich in *Life-Style Evangelism*, p. 61.

like the way I do it better than the way you don't."[3]

At one time or another, we've all fallen into one or more of these attitude traps . . . is your coffee getting low? Flag the waitress to refill your cup, and while she's coming, let's take a closer look at Jesus' words to discover some principles that may help us take a larger part in fulfilling His Great Commission.

Four Observations to Help Us Fulfill the Great Commission

Three men recorded Jesus' Great Commission in Scripture: Matthew the tax collector, John Mark the young missionary, and Luke the physician. Let's compare and analyze their accounts to make our four observations.

First: Jesus Talked to Ordinary People Who Knew Him

> The eleven disciples proceeded to Galilee, to the mountain which Jesus had designated. And when they saw Him, they worshiped Him; but some were doubtful. And Jesus came up and spoke to them, saying . . . (Matt. 28:16–18a)

> And afterward He appeared to the eleven themselves as they were reclining at the table . . . (Mark 16:14a)

> And so when they had come together . . . (Acts 1:6a)

When Jesus gave His commission, He was addressing ordinary people who knew Him well. He spoke in the most casual manner—they weren't even aware that He was giving them what we so loftily term the "Great Commission." He was simply talking to them, not pontificating at them in an orotund voice.

And those who heard His words certainly weren't heroes of the faith. "Some were doubtful," Matthew wrote (28:17). Mark said Jesus needed to reproach some for their "unbelief and hardness of heart" (16:14b). According to Luke, they had a list of questions right up to the very end (Acts 1:6a). But into the unsure hands of these doubting men, Jesus passed the baton of truth.

3. Dwight L. Moody, as told by Leighton Ford in *The Christian Persuaders* (New York, N.Y.: Harper and Row, Publishers, 1966), p. 68, as quoted by Aldrich in *Life-Style Evangelism*, p. 73.

What would they do with this baton? Jesus didn't give them any magic witnessing beans or do-it-yourself miracle kits to transform them into supermissionaries. He alone—not His followers—had been given all authority "in heaven and on earth" (Matt. 28:18). Angels didn't descend from heaven to fit the disciples with glowing halos or gleaming clerical collars. They didn't suddenly become serene saints reposing piously; they were just regular folks who knew and loved Jesus—and that's all they needed to be.

He Stated the Game Plan Deliberately and Clearly

Another observation we can make concerns Jesus' objective of spreading the gospel. "Go therefore and make disciples of all the nations," Matthew recorded (28:19a). "Go into all the world and preach the gospel to all creation," wrote Mark (16:15). Luke penned these words from Jesus:

> "You shall be My witnesses both in Jerusalem, and
> in all Judea and Samaria, and even to the remotest
> part of the earth." (Acts 1:8b)

In these statements, Jesus deliberately and clearly states the game plan—to evangelize the world. As a community of Christians, are we truly committed to this goal?

Bill and Amy Stearns, in their book *Catch the Vision 2000*, list some revealing facts:

- Roughly half of the world's population—actually about 3.05 billion—live in reached people groups. This does not mean all these individuals are Christians; it simply means they live in people groups where it's possible for them to respond to a clear presentation of the Gospel from within their own culture in their own language. . . .

- In the rest of the world, about 2.2 billion people live in unreached people groups.[4]

However, of the approximately 150,000 Christian missionaries in the world, 92 percent of them work with the reached people groups. That leaves only about 12,000 missionaries to work among

4. Bill and Amy Stearns, *Catch the Vision 2000* (Minneapolis, Minn.: Bethany House Publishers, 1991), pp. 132–33.

the 2.2 billion people who have never heard the gospel in their own language.[5]

"Manpower isn't the only area of imbalance in our attempts to make disciples of every nation," write the Stearns. Financial support for missions around the world is just as disproportionate.

> The world's believers spend 0.09% of their income on ministries to non-Christians in reached people groups, where a church movement has already been planted.
> But the world's Christians only spend 0.01% on reaching the remaining unreached people groups.[6]

These are just some facts to consider over a cup of coffee. Understanding them and the challenges they represent is the first step toward developing a compassionate heart for the world.

He Was Intense about Involvement but Relaxed regarding Method

A third observation is drawn from the action verbs Matthew, Mark, and Luke used in their accounts of Christ's Great Commission. When Jesus said, "Go," He meant what He said. We can't sit in church and wait for prospective disciples to come through the doors. We need to be active participants, personally involved in reaching out to others.

The interesting thing, however, is that Jesus didn't hand us an evangelism procedure manual. He was intense about involvement but relaxed regarding method. He mentioned "teaching" and "baptizing," but He never spelled out any exact styles, approaches, or tools. We tend to focus on methods, favoring those we've always used. But Christ allows us to use a variety of ways to get out the good news. And every link of the missionary chain is important to Him, from the home-church supporters to the printers of materials to the full-time missionaries. *Every* Christian can be involved.

This thought leads us to our final observation. Your coffee is probably getting cold, so we won't be much longer.

---

5. See Stearns, *Catch the Vision 2000*, p. 136.

6. Stearns, *Catch the Vision 2000*, p. 135.

His Command Called for Action

Jesus' commission was never meant to be simply studied; it was a call to action. Look again at the verbs: "Go . . . make disciples . . . baptizing . . . teaching" (Matt. 28:19–20); "preach" (Mark 16:15); "be My witnesses" (Acts 1:8)—energy and movement are in these words.

God may not be calling you to become a full-time missionary, but He is challenging you to participate in His Great Commission drama. He only has one script: "Go therefore and make disciples." There is no other plan.

Will you play your part?

 Living Insights

Take another look at the four common attitudes toward the Great Commission we listed in the lesson. Do any of them describe you? If so, put a check mark by the one or ones you most identify with.

❑ The attitude of specialization: "It's not my job."

❑ The attitude of isolationism: "Am I my brother's keeper?"

❑ The attitude of procrastination: "I am just too involved in other things."

❑ The attitude of rejection or indifference: "Christ found me; He can find others without my help."

The Great Commission has been on God's heart since time began. According to Genesis 12:1 and 22:15–18, what was God's worldwide goal in choosing Abraham to lead the Hebrew nation?

_____

Later in Hebrew history when Solomon built Israel's first temple, what was its purpose, according to Solomon's dedication prayer in 1 Kings 8:41–43?

_____

God promised that the Messiah would come through the Hebrew people, and "the Spirit of the Lord will rest on Him" (Isa. 11:2a).

According to chapter 49:5–6, in which the Messiah is titled "Servant," what is His purpose for coming?

_____

Simeon's blessing of baby Jesus gives us further insight into God's objectives for the world. What did Simeon wisely see in Jesus that amazed Joseph and Mary (Luke 2:25–33)?

_____

According to Jesus' words in John 3:16–17, what was the focus of His ministry?

_____

What is God's desire for the world, according to Paul's words in 1 Timothy 2:3–4?

_____

How will God's salvation scheme for the world end (Rev. 15:3–4)?

_____

Certainly, the Great Commission is just one link in the chain of God's global perspective that spans the entire Bible. In the next Living Insight, we'll examine ways we can grab hold of this chain, becoming a part of His worldwide plan.

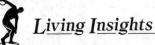

Living Insights

The world is closer than you think. Take a look at the labels on your clothing—your shirt or blouse was probably made in Korea, your trousers or skirt in Taiwan, and your shoes in Hong Kong. The fruit you ate for breakfast could have been grown in South America. Your dishes maybe came from Holland and your coffee table from Mexico.

Every day, many people around the globe indirectly touch our lives. As we become more involved in Christ's commission, we can impact their lives in return. The question is: How do we begin? The following list suggests some ways you can focus on the world.

- Invite a family from another culture over for dinner.

- Pray for people around the world, perhaps using *Operation Mobilization Prayer Cards*.[7] There is one card for every nation in the world, with pertinent prayer requests for that country.

- Adopt one of the missionary families your church sponsors. Send them letters and care packages. Host them when they are in the area, and help your children develop friendships with their kids.

- Sponsor a child through Compassion International.[8]

- House a foreign exchange student.

- Use your vacation time for a short-term mission.[9]

- Read a book on missions involvement. We recommend *How to Be a World-Class Christian*, by Paul Borthwick (Wheaton, Ill.: Scripture Press Publications, Victor Books, 1991).

- Get involved with a ministry to international students at a local college.

- Set aside some extra tithe money each month to give directly to missions.

- Consider using your skills in a foreign country. Mission organizations often need business managers, teachers, craftsmen, computer programmers, and many other professional people.

What are some ways you can start fulfilling the Great Commission from where you live?

_____

_____

The next time you see a label that begins "Made in . . . ," take a moment to pray for the people who sewed that garment or snapped together those parts. God knows their names, even though you don't. Perhaps someday they'll become Christians because you touched their lives with prayer.

7. These can be obtained from STL Books, P.O. Box 28, Waynesboro, GA 30830.

8. Post Office Box 7000, Colorado Springs, CO 80933.

9. For more information, read *Stepping Out: A Guide to Short-Term Missions* (Monrovia, Calif.: Short-Term Advocates, 1987).

Chapter 10

BREAKING WITH A BACKYARD MENTALITY

2 Corinthians 8:1–9

H ow's your appetite for adventure? Just for a moment, leave behind your televisions, telephones, and FAX machines, and travel by jet to one of the world's most exotic locales—the South American jungle. There brilliant, multicolored macaws soar freely above the mangroves, and chattering monkeys chase each other through branches high overhead. All around you, rambling mountains stretch lazily into the cloud-laced sky. Sound like paradise?

We should also tell you that there is no plumbing or electricity where you'll be staying, no drinkable water, no paved roads, no insulated houses, no central heating or air-conditioning, no supermarkets or malls, and no reliable police or government protection. You will be living among a primitive people in a strange culture, eating unnameable food, and battling insects the size of small rats. Also, because traveling through the forest is dangerous, the leech-infested river that flows nearby is your primary means of getting around. And your only connections to the outside world are a small, battery-powered two-way radio and an airplane that drops off supplies every couple of weeks. Still sound like paradise?

This is life for many tribal missionaries, who bring the gospel to the remotest parts of the world. Some of these men and women spend years translating God's Word into languages never before written, beginning at the literal beginning—deciphering the tribe's alphabet and then teaching them how to read.

Isolated, many of these missionaries face severe hardships that test them physically and emotionally. But most of them wouldn't trade their way of life for any version of earthly paradise because they've seen beyond their backyard fence and found a whole world to fill their hearts.

Beyond Our Backyard: A New Look at 2 Corinthians 8

In this portion of his letter to the Corinthians, Paul was originally addressing the matter of financial giving. However, we can gain new insights about our role as Christians in the modern world by examining some underlying themes.

A Corinthian-Macedonian Contrast

Like many of us living in North America, the Corinthians had access to it all—sophistication, education, wealth, the arts, anything they wanted to make them comfortable. But they may not have been especially concerned about those outside their direct line of vision. So Paul brought their attention to the Macedonians, a group of people who didn't have what the Corinthians considered important but had instead what God considered important.

> Now, brethren, we wish to make known to you the grace of God which has been given in the churches of Macedonia, that in a great ordeal of affliction their abundance of joy and their deep poverty overflowed in the wealth of their liberality. (vv. 1–2)

Poor, afflicted, and with less of the world's advantages than the believers in Corinth, the Macedonian churches nevertheless received the grace of God and were a lesson of joy and generosity to their privileged neighbors. In much the same way, some of our Third World brothers and sisters can be a living lesson to us.

A Macedonian-Third World Comparison

Traveling by plane, less than a day away from many of us are millions of people who, like the Macedonians, live with "a great ordeal of affliction" and "deep poverty." Guatemala, for example, ravaged by a massive earthquake in 1976, saw thousands of its people die and more than a million become instantly homeless. New pockets of poverty soon tucked themselves into surrounding regions, with families seeking shelter not only on the outlying slopes and plateaus but also along highways in dilapidated hovels made of scavenged cardboard or corrugated metal.

Yet God's grace extended even to this region, shaking the people awake to His existence and drawing those from other countries to come and tell of His healing presence. And it was here, in the midst of God's rescue work, that joy and openheartedness "overflowed" in "abundance" as people's lives were eternally transformed.

Does it surprise you to find flowering in the soil of poverty and pain the bloom of happiness? Perhaps now that we've pushed back the borders of your backyard, it's time to stretch your thinking on what missionaries are like. Because they really are some of the most fulfilled people you could ever meet.

Breaking Past Some Mental Barriers

Some of us may have spiritual gifts needed on the mission field, as well as God's unmistakable call to that ministry. However, because of false perceptions or limited knowledge, we politely decline God's open door and keep looking for one we feel will be more suitable. So let's spend some time now getting a few facts straight and broadening our ideas of who missionaries are and what they can do.

Portrait of a Missionary

Two widely divergent—and extreme—pictures seem to define "a missionary" for us: the first darkly colors him or her as weird, a fanatic, a social misfit who couldn't make it in real life. The second applies a liberal dose of gold glitter to make the missionary a supersaint—indomitable, never fatigued, abounding with enthusiasm, always aglow in prayer, the hero of heathens. Both are about as true to life as a Picasso painting.

To get a more accurate portrait, let's consider, for example, a Wycliffe translator. What skills do you think it would take to learn the ins and outs of an unknown culture? Or to master an unwritten language? And to make Scriptures relevant and understandable within the nuances of that language and people group? Let's list a few.

This type of missionary would have to be:

- well-educated
- well-read
- a linguist
- an anthropologist
- practical
- scientifically minded
- keen-thinking
- creative
- evangelical
- broad-minded
- resourceful
- deeply in love with Jesus

One other essential trait is a deep interest in the techniques of biblical interpretation. A translator daily grapples with how to convey the Bible's ideas in ways that mean something to the people they are working with, without losing any of the Scripture's meaning. Take the challenge, for example, of translating 1 Corinthians 15:58:

> Therefore, my beloved brethren, be steadfast, immovable, always abounding in the work of the Lord,

knowing that your toil is not in vain in the Lord.

What if the people you are trying to communicate with have no word for "steadfast" or "immovable"? Perhaps that part of the verse would come out something like this:

Put both your feet down on the trail. Once they have been planted, stand there, don't move.

Obviously, translation work requires creativity! It also requires a willingness to work with people from a variety of church backgrounds. Tribal translators shouldn't be too nitpicky about denominational differences. Such differences are secondary to getting the Word of God into the language of the people.

Yet translation is not the only kind of missionary work. There's a need for medical personnel who can train other missionaries not only to take care of tribal illnesses but also to take better care of themselves. Teachers, too, are vital for imparting knowledge to primitive peoples as well as instructing missionaries' children. The field is wide open—the only limit is one's imagination.

Our Best Missionary Example

Going back to 2 Corinthians, we find the epitome of the missionary heart in Jesus Himself.

For you know the grace of our Lord Jesus Christ, that though He was rich, yet for your sake He became poor, that you through His poverty might become rich. (8:9)

From the infinite wealth of heaven, Christ willingly joined our human poverty—poverty of mind, of spirit, of heart, of soul. He disrobed Himself of the privileges of deity to put on the limitations of our frail flesh. And He lived with us and died for us so that we could exchange our poverty for the richness of His life.

Two Prodding Questions

Being a foreign missionary is not for everyone, but it is for some. Before you make up your mind, carefully consider these two questions: (1) Have you become strangely discontented, restless, and dissatisfied in your work? (2) Are you unsure about your career or where you're going after completing school? Perhaps missions is the answer God is trying to get you to see. Why not try a short-term mission project to test whether you have the gifts and the God-given direction?

Of course, Christ may not be calling you into full-time missionary work. If you're right where you ought to be, take time to ask God what you could do to play a decisive part in His world program. Move beyond your own backyard by finding some creative ways to invest your time and resources in fulfilling the Great Commission in your neighborhood, in your city, and in your world.

 Living Insights

Some people say with a sigh, "Missions is for the young and energetic. I used to be that way, but now I'm older; my ways are set and my roots run too deep to try something new."

General Douglas MacArthur has something to say to people like that.

> Youth is not a period of time. It is a state of mind, a result of the will, a quality of the imagination, a victory of courage over timidity, of the taste for adventure over the love of comfort. A man does not grow old simply because he has lived a certain number of years. A man becomes old when he has deserted his ideal. The years wrinkle his skin, but deserting his ideal wrinkles his soul. Preoccupations, fears, doubts and despair are the enemies which slowly bow us toward earth, and turn us into dust before death. You will remain young as long as you are receptive to what is beautiful, good, great; receptive to the messages of men and women, of nature and of God. If one day you should become bitter and pessimistic and gnawed by despair, may God have mercy on your old man's soul.[1]

Based on these powerful words, can we ask you a few personal questions, as gently as possible? Over the years, has your love of comfort overtaken your taste for adventure? Has the Lord's ideal

---

1. Douglas MacArthur, as quoted by Brennan Manning in *The Signature of Jesus* (Portland, Oreg.: Multnomah Press, 1992), pp. 170—71.

for your life grown distant? Are wrinkles cropping up in your soul? In short, are you getting old?

We encourage you to formulate—or reformulate—your life ideal. It may not be translating the Bible for some remote jungle tribe, but it should reflect the talents God has given you and the part you can play in glorifying Him and fulfilling His Great Commission.

The following steps, outlined by Charles Bradshaw and Dave Gilbert in their book *Too Hurried to Love*, are designed to help you discover your purpose in life. Before you begin, though, read Paul's life ideal in Acts 20:24, and use it to shape your own thoughts.

"What are the twelve things you enjoy doing the most?"

_____

_____

_____

_____

"What are some of the hurts, problems, and needs you see in your world and would like to help solve?"

_____

_____

_____

"Do you want God to be at the center of your life and purpose? Why?"

_____

_____

_____

"What do you and your friends see as your ten greatest strengths or talents?"

_____

_____

_____

"What do you want printed on your tombstone?"

_____

_____

_____

Now formulate your life ideal by completing the following sentence: "I exist to . . ."[2]

_____

_____

_____

In the Lord's strength, follow your dream. And never, never let your heart grow old.

Living Insights

How does your life ideal relate to your career? The following chart helps us define these two concepts.

Life Ideal	Career
Overall Purpose	Specific Pathway
Divine Calling	Earthly Course
Vision	Task
Vocation	Occupation

Distinguishing the two even further, Ben Patterson writes,

> Our vocation is our calling to serve Christ; our occupations are the jobs we do to earn our way in the world. While it is our calling to press our occupations into the service of our vocation, it is idolatrous to equate the two. Happy is the man or woman

2. See Charles Bradshaw and Dave Gilbert, _Too Hurried to Love_ (Eugene, Oreg.: Harvest House Publishers, 1991), pp. 50–51.

whose vocation and occupations come close. But it is no disaster if they do not.

If tomorrow I am fired from my job as pastor of New Providence Presbyterian Church and am forced to find employment in the Sunoco station down the street, my vocation would remain intact. I still would be called to preach. Nothing would have changed my call substantially, just the situation in which I obey it.[3]

After pondering your life ideal in the previous Living Insight, you may have discovered that your vocation or calling in life does not match your occupation. Perhaps, then, you need to change your career, or maybe you just need to change your perspective toward your career. Whether your job right now is managing a business, driving a truck, or caring for children, how can you begin to express your life ideal through your career?

_____

_____

_____

In what ways can you "break the boundaries of your backyard," expressing your life ideal in the world?

_____

_____

_____

In uncertain days when many people lose their jobs, it is reassuring to know God never lays off His workers. For

> we are His workmanship, created in Christ Jesus for good works, which God prepared beforehand, that we should walk in them. (Eph. 2:10)

He has prepared you to accomplish His calling in your life. No matter what occupation changes occur, hold fast to your life ideal, and never let your vision fade.

3. Ben Patterson, "Is Ministry a Career?" in *Leadership*, Summer 1990, p. 55.

Chapter 11

GOLD IN THE MAKING

Job 23:3–14

```
          RECIPE FOR MAKING GOLD

1 clump mined ore
soda
borax
pinch of silica
dash of lead oxide
flour

Grind the ore until it is a fine powder. Add the
remaining ingredients and mix well. Heat mixture
until lead becomes molten and picks up the
precious metals in the ore. Cool slowly until
solidified into a small lead button. Drop into a
special porous cup, and place the cup into another
high-temperature furnace. Fire up the furnace
until lead liquefies and soaks into the porous
cup. The remaining tiny metal bead will be a
mixture of gold and silver. Remove bead, clean
thoroughly, pound it flat, and roll it out into a
thin strip. Treat with nitric acid to remove
silver content. Yield: one flake of solid gold.
```

What does it take to refine gold from ore? Grinding, mixing, melting, scrubbing, pounding, rolling, and treating with acid—not a pleasant procedure from the ore's point of view.

Neither is it an enjoyable process when the trials of life grind and melt and pound us. But God uses them to refine golden character qualities in our lives. What, then, can help us endure trial's furnace? What hope does God offer us?

Our ancient friend Job certainly felt the pain of refinement. The principles we quarry from his example can prepare us to endure tribulation's fire and emerge less like ordinary ore and more like gleaming gold. Let's sit with him for awhile in his crucible of misery and listen as he bares his soul to the Lord.

This chapter, as well as the next one, elaborates on the general topics that we introduced in chapter 4, "The Crowns of Righteousness and Life."

A Brief Review of Job's Predicament

Job has lost everything dear to him: his livelihood, his possessions, his servants, and his children (Job 1:13–19). He has even lost his health, stricken by Satan with boils "from the sole of his foot to the crown of his head" (2:7). Crushed physically and devastated emotionally, poor Job now just shakes his head in bewilderment, wondering why such tragedies would happen to one who had followed God faithfully and blamelessly. Still,

> through all this Job did not sin nor did he blame God. (1:22)

Four of his friends have come to console him, but their words of comfort soon turn into heavy-handed advice. Feeling shut off from God, misunderstood and attacked by his so-called counselors, and lost in an endless tunnel of troubles, Job utters a heartfelt "if only."

Job's Desire

> Then Job replied,
> "Even today my complaint is rebellion;
> His hand is heavy despite my groaning.
> Oh that I knew where I might find Him,
> That I might come to His seat!
> I would present my case before Him
> And fill my mouth with arguments.
> I would learn the words which He would answer,
> And perceive what He would say to me.
> Would He contend with me by the greatness of His
>   power?
> No, surely He would pay attention to me.
> There the upright would reason with Him;
> And I would be delivered forever from my Judge."
> (23:1–7)

Just like us during difficult days, Job longs to talk face-to-face with God, if even for a few minutes. There God would be, listening attentively, as a father to his child. On the edge of His great throne, He would lean forward with His chin in His hands, nodding empathetically while Job poured out his anguish. "Why, Lord? How long?" Surely God would offer him some answers, and Job would have some relief.

But God seems nowhere to be found, and Job's heart churns with frustration.

> "Behold, I go forward but He is not there,
> And backward, but I cannot perceive Him;
> When He acts on the left, I cannot behold Him;
> He turns on the right, I cannot see Him."
> (vv. 8–9)

All he perceives is the trial in his life—God grinding and pounding him in a painful ordeal. Until, from behind the heavenly mist, Job remembers three reassuring truths about his sovereign Judge.

A Respite of Reassurance

He Knows My Way

In contrast to his frustrated efforts to find God, Job writes hopefully,

> "But He knows the way I take." (v. 10a)

Although he is unable to comprehend God's ways, Job is sure of this truth: *God knows his way.*

The Hebrew word for *way*, *derek*, has a broader meaning than just "the path I am taking" or "the things that are happening to me." It is related to the verb *darak*, which means "tread"—a word sometimes used as a Hebrew idiom for treading or stepping on the bow to bend and string it.[1] So we could translate the verse as, "He knows the way I am bent—He knows how I'm made, my characteristics and my personality."[2]

The psalmist echoes Job's words:

> O Lord, Thou hast searched me and known me.
> Thou dost know when I sit down and when I rise up;
> Thou dost understand my thought from afar.
> Thou dost scrutinize my path and my lying down,

---

1. Herbert Wolf, "darak," in *Theological Wordbook of the Old Testament,* ed. R. Laird Harris, Gleason L. Archer, Jr., Bruce K. Waltke (Chicago, Ill.: Moody Press, 1980), vol. 1, p. 196.

2. See also Proverbs 22:6a, "Train up a child in the way he should go," and 30:19, "The way of an eagle in the sky, The way of a serpent on a rock, The way of a ship in the middle of the sea, And the way of a man with a maid." These verses use the word *way* to describe mannerisms and characteristics.

And art intimately acquainted with all my *ways*.
(Ps. 139:1–3, emphasis added)

God knows us inside and out. In fact, the word translated "intimately acquainted," *sakan*, literally means to "be of use or service, benefit."[3] He knows what benefits us; therefore, He is able to shape our character with our best interests in mind.

He Refines My Way

The process He employs in shaping us is the subject of the next truth Job describes. He writes, "He has tried me"—stated another way, *He refines my way* (Job 23:10b). Not satisfied just to know our ways, the Lord takes it upon Himself to burn off the sinful dross and form a character of pure gold.

Because of our sinfulness, this refining process requires the Lord's relentless searching and testing. According to the prophet Jeremiah,

"The heart is more deceitful than all else
And is desperately sick;
Who can understand it?
I, the Lord, search the heart,
I test the mind,
Even to give to each man according to his ways,
According to the results of his deeds."
(Jer. 17:9–10)

However, God is not trying to destroy us through testing. Another prophet, Isaiah, assures us that God will be with us:

"When you pass through the waters, I will be with
    you;
And through the rivers, they will not overflow you.
When you walk through the fire, you will not be
    scorched,
Nor will the flame burn you . . .
Since you are precious in My sight,
Since you are honored and I love you."
(Isa. 43:2, 4a)

God does not design our trials to drown or devour us. His intent is to bring out our best.

---

3. William Gesenius, *A Hebrew and English Lexicon of the Old Testament*, trans. Edward Robinson, (Oxford, England: Clarendon Press, n.d.), p. 698.

He Guarantees Greater Value as a Result

Job concludes, "I shall come forth as gold" (23:10c), revealing a third truth: *He guarantees greater value as a result.* Notice that Job says "I shall," not "I hope" or "I might." Trials *will* bring out the gold in our lives—gold that is now present in raw form.

"The fire does not change gold but exposes the substance already there," observes Henry Gariepy.

> Trial and affliction similarly bring out the quality already present in a life. As pure gold shines all the brighter when put to the fire, so faith glows the more radiant when put to the fiery test. In the end, Job's faith and trust, which already had made him a model in God's sight, enabled him to "come forth as gold."[4]

Those refined qualities of faith and trust increase our usefulness to God, because now we can serve Him in ways we could not have imagined before our trials. Of what use is a clump of ore? A doorstop maybe. But think of the versatility of durable, malleable, glimmering gold! That is the far more valuable product God wants to develop in our lives—a product whose raw material already resides within us.

Job's Response

Having recalled God's reassurance, Job responds to these truths in two ways. First, he states that he will not stray from the Lord even though the refining process is painful.

> "My foot has held fast to His path;
> I have kept His way and not turned aside.
> I have not departed from the command of His lips."
> (vv. 11–12a)

How easy it is for us to desert the Lord during trials. Pain can cause us to run in desperation and fear or scream back at God in anger, and we start wanting our own way rather than His way. Job looks back and says confidently, "I have kept His way." And he determines to walk even closer to the Lord in the heat of his trial's furnace, developing an ultrasensitive spirit of obedience in the process.

---

4. Henry Gariepy, *Portraits of Perseverance* (Wheaton, Ill.: Scripture Press Publications, Victor Books, 1989), p. 127.

Second, he decides to listen to what the Lord says, developing an ultrasensitive ear of attention. He states,

> "I have treasured the words of His mouth more than
> my necessary food." (v. 12b)

During hard times, we need to be quiet and still in order to hear the Lord's voice. The temptation is to busy ourselves worrying about and trying to work out our problems. Job, however, centers his thoughts on God's Word. Because the Lord speaks to us through our trials, we should make a special effort to listen.

What Happens Next?

Eventually, the time of testing will end. What happens then? Can we rest, hoping to never endure another trial? Job's next observation answers that.

> "He is unique and who can turn Him?
> And what His soul desires, that He does.
> For He performs what is appointed for me,
> And many such decrees are with Him."
> (vv. 13–14)

"Many such decrees" means that many more trials are "with Him"! Our *derek* constantly needs God's attention, so He is perpetually purifying, honing, and molding us. We truly can rejoice in the midst of trials, not because we anticipate relief someday, but because God is making something more valuable out of our lives. We are gold in the making!

Living Insights STUDY ONE

Henry Gariepy describes the precious insights trials provide us:

> The Arabs have a proverb: "All sunshine makes
> a desert." (They ought to know.) When life is easy,
> it is possible to live on the surface of things. But
> when trial and sorrow come, then one is driven to
> the deeper things. Then one can enter into the se-
> crets and beauties of God. It is in the storm that
> God arches His rainbow over us, its multi-splendor
> revealing all the elements of color that make up the

beauty of the world. Life's greatest revelations come in its storms.[5]

Like a six-year-old watching a monster movie, though, we tend to bury our eyes in our hands when an ugly trial jumps into the scene. As a result, we miss the best parts of life's unfolding drama!

If you're enduring a hard time, you may not be able to see any good coming out of it because it's all too scary right now. But, when the lights come on and the credits roll, you'll probably have a better perspective of "the deeper things" Gariepy is talking about. Until then, peek through your fingers and look intently at your trial. Then take a few moments to be quiet and listen to the Lord's still voice.

What rainbow revelations is He arching before you concerning your life? Your priorities? Your goals? Your relationships? Take a few moments to think. We'll provide you some space to write down what you discover.

_____

_____

_____

_____

_____

_____

Living Insights

While enduring stormy trials, the last thing we want is an earful of sunny clichés from friends sailing smoothly through life. "Look on the bright side," they'll say. "Every cloud has a silver lining." "When life gives you a lemon, make lemonade." Or, "Cheer up, it could be worse." That's encouraging?

Clichéd advice is about as helpful as an umbrella in a hurricane. Scripture verses can even sound trite at times like these. One verse too often tossed about glibly is Romans 8:28:

And we know that God causes all things to work

---

5. Gariepy, *Portraits of Perseverance*, pp. 127–28.

together for good to those who love God, to those
who are called according to His purpose.

Despite its sometimes insensitive use, this verse does contain a
wealth of helpful truth that can provide a sturdy shelter.

Let's examine it in its context. Verses 26–28 address the relationship between us and God when we're weak and do not even
know how to pray. During these times, what does the Holy Spirit
do on our behalf?

_____

_____

Who does "He" refer to in verse 27 (see also verse 34)? What
is His role when we are weak?

_____

_____

In verse 28, we discover God the Father's behind-the-scenes
work for us. Notice that "He causes all things to work *together*." In
your life, how has God drawn from different experiences—some
pleasant, some unpleasant—to work together for good? For example, think how the gold refined during a previous trial is strengthening you now.

_____

_____

_____

What is God's ultimate good that He promises for those who
love Him (vv. 29–30)?

_____

_____

The remainder of Romans 8 paints a striking portrait of God's
undying love for us:

Neither death, nor life, nor angels, nor principalities,
nor things present, nor things to come, nor powers,

> nor height, nor depth, nor any other created thing,
> shall be able to separate us from the love of God,
> which is in Christ Jesus our Lord. (vv. 38b–39)

Has God abandoned you in your sorrow? No. He is there, groaning with you, interceding for you, and working behind-the-scenes in ways you may not yet understand. During your hardship, we encourage you not to stray from His love. You may not comprehend all His ways—but you can see His love, etched in tears on your Savior's face.

Chapter 12

WHERE IS GOD
WHEN WE HURT?

Isaiah 41:1–10

A uthor C. S. Lewis was more than fifty years old when he finally
fell in love. The woman who captured his bachelor heart was
Joy Davidman, an American writer. On April 23, 1956, they married, but tragically, four years later she died from cancer. In his journal, published under the title *A Grief Observed*, Lewis poured out
his tears in words that expressed the depth of his loneliness and grief.

> Meanwhile, where is God? This is one of the most
> disquieting symptoms [of grief]. When you are happy,
> so happy that you have no sense of needing Him,
> so happy that you are tempted to feel His claims
> upon you as an interruption, if you remember yourself and turn to Him with gratitude and praise, you
> will be—or so it feels—welcomed with open arms.
> But go to Him when your need is desperate, when
> all other help is vain, and what do you find? A door
> slammed in your face, and a sound of bolting and
> double bolting on the inside. After that, silence. You
> may as well turn away. The longer you wait, the
> more emphatic the silence will become. There are
> no lights in the windows. It might be an empty
> house. Was it ever inhabited? It seemed so once.
> And that seeming was as strong as this. What can
> this mean? Why is He so present a commander in
> our time of prosperity and so very absent a help in
> time of trouble?[1]

Where *is* God when we hurt? Has He locked Himself away in
His celestial castle? Has He suddenly become too busy with more
pressing matters? In our pain, many of us have pondered these
questions, but few have put them into words so eloquent or bold

---

1. C. S. Lewis, *A Grief Observed* (New York, N.Y.: Bantam Books, 1961), pp. 4–5.

as C. S. Lewis. Is God absent or, as Psalm 46:1 contends, "a very present help in trouble"? Let's turn to Isaiah 41 to try to find some answers.

A Brief Look at the Context

In order to fully appreciate Isaiah's words, we'll need to understand their context. The people of Judah are in trouble; churning on the horizon are the storm clouds of God's judgment—because God's people have turned their backs on Him, an idolatrous kingdom, Babylon, will eventually conquer them and carry the nation into exile.

Still, God won't turn His back on them. In verse 2, Isaiah makes reference to "one from the east," generally believed to be Cyrus, king of Persia, who will end Judah's exile in Babylon.

With this background in mind, we can divide our passage into two sections: verses 1–7 are addressed to Judah's enemies, and verses 8–10 are words of comfort and reassurance to Judah. Let's look at the first section and see common responses to affliction.

Common Responses to Affliction

> "Coastlands, listen to Me in silence,
> And let the peoples gain new strength;
> Let them come forward, then let them speak;
> Let us come together for judgment.
> Who has aroused one from the east
> Whom He calls in righteousness to His feet?
> He delivers up nations before him,
> And subdues kings.
> He makes them like dust with his sword,
> As the wind-driven chaff with his bow.
> He pursues them, passing on in safety,
> By a way he had not been traversing with his feet.
> Who has performed and accomplished it,
> Calling forth the generations from the beginning?
> 'I, the Lord, am the first, and with the last. I am He.'"
> (Isa. 41:1–4)

Here God challenges the nations who captured and oppressed Judah to come and see the judgment He has in store for them. He is arousing Cyrus to conquer them, making them "like dust with his sword" and "as the wind-driven chaff with his bow." Later in the book, Isaiah even mentions him by name (see 44:28–45:7).

Let's listen in as the prophet then observes the nations' reactions to this chilling prediction, the first of which is *fear and trembling.*

> The coastlands have seen and are afraid;
> The ends of the earth tremble;
> They have drawn near and have come.
> (41:5)

Their fear draws the people to one place, where they exhibit a second response: *mutual encouragement.* Hoping to cheer one another on, they try to use positive-thinking techniques to bolster their courage.

> Each one helps his neighbor,
> And says to his brother, "Be strong!"
> (v. 6)

"Be strong," they cry out to one another, but their voices waver as the skies grow darker. Rather than running to God for help, though, their third reaction is to turn to *superstition.*

> So the craftsman encourages the smelter,
> And he who smooths metal with the hammer
>   encourages him who beats the anvil,
> Saying of the soldering, "It is good";
> And he fastens it with nails,
> That it should not totter.
> (v. 7)

In the face of calamity, the people hurriedly construct an idol, saying when it is completed, "It is good—it will protect us." They are grasping desperately for something to hang on to in the impending storm.

How do we respond when threatened by affliction? Our natural reactions are often modern versions of the three that Isaiah observed in the pagan nations. Who hasn't felt a flush of fear when, for example, the doctor says, "You need surgery right away"? And who hasn't tried to calm the trembling through cheery optimism and positive thinking? And when the pressure mounts, who hasn't grasped for security by superstitiously crossing fingers, knocking on wood, or repeating formulated prayers?

When we find ourselves reacting in these ways, it is helpful to shift our focus from our affliction to our Lord. Isaiah reassures us that God is not idle during our suffering. He is actively doing His part.

God's Part When We Suffer

While enduring pain, we often have difficulty seeing God's actions through our tears. Sometimes, what helps us see Him at work is to look at ourselves and our problems from His perspective.

The Perspective He Offers

God's words of comfort to Judah in verses 8–10 show us that the Lord views His people in a unique light.

> "But you, Israel, My servant,
> Jacob whom I have chosen,
> Descendant of Abraham My friend,
> You whom I have taken from the ends of the earth,
> And called from its remotest parts,
> And said to you, 'You are My servant,
> I have chosen you and not rejected you.'"
> (vv. 8–9)

When storms arise, we wonder: Is He punishing us? Has He left us to wander as orphans through our affliction? Has He abandoned us? But according to the Lord's words through Isaiah, He has not rejected us. He has chosen us, taken us, and called us—what reassurance there is in these words!

Since He has claimed us as His own, He would never turn His back on us, even though our feelings tell us otherwise. Actually, if we look at our situations from His perspective, our trials prove His love. A problem-free life would make our fallen souls spiritually dull and insensitive, yet how responsive and mature we can become through hardship! Alexander Solzhenitsyn, a Russian dissident who was imprisoned in Siberia for his writings, was even thankful for his suffering because of what it taught him.

> It was only when I lay there on rotting prison straw that I sensed within myself the first stirrings of good. Gradually, it was disclosed to me that the line separating good and evil passes, not through states, nor between classes, nor between political parties either, but right through every human heart, and through

all human hearts. So, bless you, prison, for having been in my life.[2]

This point of view is similar to a woman's perspective after giving birth—the excruciating labor was worth it for the joy that came after. But during the pain, what is God doing? Where is God when we hurt?

The Action He Takes

The first line of verse 10 gives us the answer: "Do not fear, for I am with you." When we cry, He is there holding our hands. When we pound on His door and hear no answer, it is not because He is busy inside; He is outside on the doorstep with us, only our fear is like a fog, misting our vision of Him and keeping us from reaching out in trust.

To His trembling children, God says,

> "'Do not anxiously look about you, for I am your
> God.
> I will strengthen you, surely I will help you,
> Surely I will uphold you with My righteous right
> hand.'" (v. 10b)

He gently bolsters our confidence by reassuring us, "I am your God—I haven't lost control. I'm still all-powerful." As Almighty God, He tells us what He will do for us.

First, *I will strengthen you*. The Hebrew word for "strengthen," *amets*, means literally, "to make firm." Commentator F. Delitzsch defines the word further: "to attach firmly to one's self."[3] We might imagine ourselves as a thread wrapped around by the steel cords of a heavy-duty cable. By ourselves, we would fear the slightest pull; but strengthened by the cable, we can stand up to greater pressure.

Second, *I will help you*. Having strengthened us, God promises to assist us through the trial. Interestingly, the same Hebrew word was used in verse 6 for people trying to help each other cope with hardship. How much more able is God's help in times of trouble!

---

2. Alexander Solzhenitsyn, as quoted by Philip Yancey in *Where Is God When It Hurts* (Grand Rapids, Mich.: Zondervan Publishing House, 1977), p. 51.

3. F. Delitzsch, *Isaiah*, vol. 7 of Commentary on the Old Testament series, by C. F. Keil and F. Delitzsch, trans. James Martin (reprint; Grand Rapids, Mich.: William B. Eerdmans Publishing Co., 1978), p. 163.

Third, *I will uphold you. Tamak* in Hebrew means to "hold up, support." Combining this idea with the previous two, God is saying, "I will attach Myself to you to strengthen you; I will help you through your trial; and when it gets so difficult that you can't make it any further, I will lift you up and carry you."

Depicting God's upholding grace in our lives is the familiar "One Set of Footprints."

> One night a man had a dream. He dreamed he was walking along the beach with the Lord. Across the sky flashed scenes from his life. For each scene he noticed two sets of footprints in the sand—one belonging to him and the other to the Lord. When the last scene had flashed before him, he looked back at the footprints and noticed that many times along the path there was only one set of footprints in the sand. He also noticed that this happened during the lowest and saddest times in his life. This really bothered him and he questioned the Lord: "Lord, you said that once I decided to follow You, You would walk all the way, but I noticed that during the most troublesome times of my life, there was only one set of footprints. I don't understand why, when I needed you most, you deserted me." The Lord replied: "My precious, precious child, I love you and would never leave you. During your times of trial and suffering when you see only one set of footprints, it was then that I carried you."[4]

Has God deserted us when we need Him most? Is pain's path ours to travel alone? "Do not fear," answers the Lord. "I am your God, and I am with you."

 Living Insights

> "Behold, the virgin shall be with child, and shall bear a Son, and they shall call His name Immanuel," which translated means, "God with us." (Matt. 1:23)

4. Author unknown.

When God became a man, He didn't parade His perfection; He became one of us. And, ultimately, God's "with-ness" is the only lasting solution to the problem of pain—at least, it's the only solution we can understand. We may not be able to explain to a child why her daddy left; we may not know the good that can come from a young bride's cancer; we may not perceive the reasons why one godly couple is childless, while thousands of precious babies are born to abusive parents. There may be no better reason than the fact that we live in an ugly, sin-infested world. But what keeps us from despair is realizing that Jesus suffered too. God felt pain!

Peter Kreeft elaborates the meaning of that truth for us.

> He came. He entered space and time and suffering. He came, like a lover. Love seeks above all intimacy, presence, togetherness. . . . He came. That is the salient fact, the towering truth, that alone keeps us from putting a bullet through our heads. He came. Job is satisfied even though the God who came gave him absolutely no answers at all to his thousand tortured questions. He did the most important thing and he gave the most important gift: himself. It is a lover's gift. Out of our tears, our waiting, our darkness, our agonized aloneness, out of our weeping and wondering, out of our cry, "My God, my God, why hast Thou forsaken me?" he came, all the way, right into that cry.[5]

Jesus is the eloquence of God's love—"the Word" that became flesh and dwelt among us (John 1:14). Christ will dwell with you in your sorrow if you seek Him in your tears.

Before reading the next Living Insight, set aside the study guide for a few moments and search your soul. What are your hurts and your disappointments? Where have you suffered? How have you been spat upon, insulted, or mocked? After a time of being honest with your pain, read Jesus' passion in John 19. Let Him, from the cross, melt your anxiety and wipe away your tears.

5. Peter Kreeft, *Making Sense Out of Suffering* (Ann Arbor, Mich.: Servant Books, 1986), p. 133.

Living Insights

Like Peter walking on—then sinking in—the water (see Matt. 14:29–31), our response to storms in life is often fear, not faith. And, many times, we sink even quicker because our pockets are heavy with excuses for not trusting God. Here's a list of some of them; check the ones you recognize in yourself.

❏ I prayed for God's help in the past, but things turned out worse.

❏ I've learned the only person I can trust is myself.

❏ God's too busy to be concerned with my problems.

❏ I can handle it on my own.

❏ Why should I try when I know I'll fail?

❏ How can I trust God when He allows so much suffering in the world?

❏ I'm no saint—I feel like a hypocrite praying for God's help.

❏ I'm mad at God.

Are there any other reasons you have difficulty trusting God? Take a moment to write them down.

_____

_____

Admitting and examining our excuses usually weakens their weighty power in our lives. Take a few moments to talk to the Lord in prayer concerning these trust-sinkers in your heart. Ask Him to help you place your whole faith in Him so that He can strengthen, assist, and uphold you during your present storm. The following space is provided for you to write down your prayer, if you wish.

_____

_____

_____

_____

Chapter 13

RESTORING RESPECT FOR THE MINISTRY

Selected Scriptures

Extra, extra!" shouts the newsboy. "'Preacher Caught in Hotel Love Nest.' Read all about it!" The boy holds up a newspaper for passersby to view the disgraceful pictures. "'Minister Locked Up for Pocketing Parish Funds.' Story inside!" continues the young town crier. "'Religious Leader Orders Mass Suicide.' Getcha paper here. Only 25 cents."

Scandal, shame, and tragedy—that's what sells newspapers. Not too long ago, the front-page faces were of non-Christian celebrities, politicians, and criminals. Today though, Christian leaders occupy the headlines with increasing frequency. These people have genuinely loved God, their families, and their congregations, but they've listened to the Pied Piper of secret sin and followed it to their own destruction, the devastation of their families, and the collapse of their ministries. As a result, along with the sprawling headlines, mud has been flung on the name of Christ and the high calling of the pastoral ministry.

Of course, no minister is sinless. And even though the ministry has always been built on the uncompromising pillars of godliness, integrity, and purity, God has never required perfection from pastors. The apostle Paul certainly wasn't perfect, and he was the first to admit it:

> I was formerly a blasphemer and a persecutor and a violent aggressor. And yet I was shown mercy, because I acted ignorantly in unbelief; and the grace of our Lord was more than abundant, with the faith and love which are found in Christ Jesus. It is a trustworthy statement, deserving full acceptance, that Christ Jesus came into the world to save sinners, among whom I am foremost of all. (1 Tim. 1:13–15)

This chapter elaborates on the general topics that we introduced in chapter 5, "The Unfading Crown of Glory."

Although Paul was fallible, before and after his conversion, he never brought shame to His Lord—like some ministers have recently. Today, it seems the world has less respect for the pastoral ministry and the church than at any other time in history. Warren Wiersbe laments:

> After a good deal of thought, I've come to the conclusion that the one word that best describes the evangelical church situation today is *reproach*. . . .
> . . . Evangelical Christians today are not like a group of schoolchildren, standing around blushing because we were caught breaking the rules. We are more like a defeated army, naked before our enemies, and unable to fight back because they have made a frightening discovery: the church is lacking in integrity.[1]

According to Wiersbe, the roles of the church and the world have reversed ironically.

> For nineteen centuries, the church has been telling the world to admit its sins, repent, and believe the gospel. Today, in the twilight of the twentieth century, the world is telling the church to face up to her sins, repent, *and start being the true church of that gospel.* We Christians boast that we are not ashamed of the gospel of Christ, but perhaps the gospel of Christ is ashamed of us. For some reason, our ministry doesn't match our message. . . .
> The church has grown accustomed to hearing people question the *message* of the gospel, because that message is foolishness to the lost. But today the situation is embarrassingly reversed, for now the *messenger* is suspect. Both the ministry and the message of the church have lost credibility before a watching world, and the world seems to be enjoying the spectacle.[2]

1. Warren W. Wiersbe, *The Integrity Crisis*, exp. ed. (Nashville, Tenn.: Thomas Nelson Publishers, Oliver Nelson, 1991), pp. 16–17.

2. Wiersbe, *The Integrity Crisis*, pp. 17–18.

How did the church and its leaders drift off course into these swirling backwaters of shame and disgrace? If we briefly review the church's recent past, we can retrace our tack into trouble and begin to navigate a new course toward restoring respect for the ministry.

Realistic Glimpses of the Shameful Scene

During the Vietnam War in the 1960s and 1970s, the ministry lost face when young men enrolled in seminary to avoid the draft. In the late 1970s, the horrible Jonestown mass suicide shocked the world with the power of religious brainwashing.

With the 1980s came the electronic church and the rise of the televangelist. Unscrupulous fund-raising techniques became acceptable; and as cash poured in, some maverick ministers began dipping into the money pot to subsidize personal excesses. The PTL incident was an example of this kind of fraud; combined with a sex scandal, it made for juicy tabloid headlines.

An epidemic of immorality has continued spreading across denominational lines and across all levels of the church. Pastor Ted Kitchens, in his book *Aftershock*, states that he has "personally witnessed the fall of: twenty Christian couples, ten pastors, [and] two seminary professors."[3] You probably have your own list of Christians you know who have forfeited their integrity for money, power, or passion.

Unfortunately, the fallout of each man or woman's moral failure is not limited to themselves alone.

> Even ministries of integrity are now being viewed with suspicion. . . . Everybody is fair game. Perhaps the saddest dimension of all are the innocent lives close to those who have fallen and failed so scandalously. I'm thinking of whole church congregations who must go on after discovering that their minister lived deceitfully in immorality. Think also of the faculty members and students who are left in the wake of a president or some campus leader who brought reproach to the name of Christ. And how about the mate and children who have to pick up

3. Ted Kitchens, *Aftershock: What to Do When Leaders and Others Fail You* (Portland, Oreg.: Multnomah Press, 1992), p. 15.

the pieces because of their husband's and father's careless and selfish indulgence? And don't forget fellow church-staff personnel whose future is uncertain because their leader lived a lie.[4]

In many ways, the consequences of sin have run the ministry aground. But now is the time to take action, to launch the ship out of the shallows of disrespect and steer her back into the high seas of integrity. For the remainder of the chapter we wish to be like Paul, who unflinchingly addressed the hypocrisy of the church's apostates but still had encouraging words for his pastor friend Timothy:

> But the Spirit explicitly says that in later times some will fall away from the faith, paying attention to deceitful spirits and doctrines of demons, by means of the hypocrisy of liars seared in their own conscience as with a branding iron, men who forbid marriage and advocate abstaining from foods, which God has created to be gratefully shared in by those who believe and know the truth. For everything created by God is good, and nothing is to be rejected, if it is received with gratitude; for it is sanctified by means of the word of God and prayer.
> In pointing out these things to the brethren, you will be a good servant of Christ Jesus, constantly nourished on the words of the faith and of the sound doctrine which you have been following. (1 Tim. 4:1–6)

While pointing out the failings we see in today's church, we desire to awaken you to the importance of being a "good servant of Christ Jesus." Here are some facts that will help you and your church leaders restore respect for the ministry.

Helpful Facts That Are Easily Forgotten

First, *Scripture predicts and warns us of such times.* Paul specifically forewarned us of the epidemic proportions of immorality in the last days:

> But realize this, that in the last days difficult

4. Charles R. Swindoll, *Rise and Shine: A Wake-Up Call* (Portland, Oreg.: Multnomah Press, 1989), p. 223.

times will come. For men will be lovers of self, lovers of money, boastful, arrogant, revilers, disobedient to parents, ungrateful, unholy, unloving, irreconcilable, malicious gossips, without self-control, brutal, haters of good, treacherous, reckless, conceited, lovers of pleasure rather than lovers of God; holding to a form of godliness, although they have denied its power; and avoid such men as these. (2 Tim. 3:1–5)

These sins read like a typical television miniseries script! They've almost lost their shock appeal, they're so pervasive. While being careful not to become callous to these evils, we should not be overwhelmed or surprised when we see the escalating effects of sin, especially in the church. They prove all the more that Christ's coming is near, and that fact should motivate us to live each day in light of His glorious arrival (see also Matt. 24:4–14, 23–25; Jude 17–21).

Second, *the actual percentage of those in ministry who fall is quite small.* Although evil is on the rise, most men and women in the ministry remain morally inculpable. The problem is, the faithful majority do not get as much press as the fallen few. Chuck Colson observed this discrepancy while being interviewed on secular radio and television talk shows about his book *Kingdoms in Conflict.*

This day's session was typical. "Today we're interviewing Charles Colson," my host said smoothly. "But first, let's hear from 'God's little goofballs.'" With that he flipped a switch, and a prerecorded message from Jim and Tammy Bakker filled the studio. I'm not sure, but I think the inspirational recording included Tammy's recipe for three-layer bean dip. The interviewer grinned. "And now, we have another evangelist with us today. Let's hear what Chuck Colson has to say."

The majority of my nearly 100 interviews began in a similar manner. Christian-bashing is very much in fashion these days. The Bakker affair has produced a comic caricature of all Christians and derision that runs deeper than most of us realize.

At first I was defensive. But as the interviews continued I got angry. What about the 350,000 churches across America where people's needs are quietly being met? I asked. The thousands of missionaries to the poor, the army of Christian volunteers who faithfully go into prisons each week? Why does the media focus instead on the flamboyant few? It's not fair, I argued, to stereotype the whole church; we're not all hypocrites out to pad our pockets.

But my interviewer simply smiled. Reason, after all, is no match for ridicule.[5]

Most Christian leaders are trustworthy and are faithfully serving Christ. If we lose sight of that fact, we may sink into despair like Elijah, who moaned to the Lord, "I alone am left" (1 Kings 19:14). Rather, be encouraged—for every fallen star there are thousands of others that may not attract as much attention but are shining for Christ in today's dark sky.

Third, *human imperfection includes ministers*. In fact, the Bible is full of imperfect saints. Let's list just a few of them:

- Noah, who was drunk and indecently exposed
- Aaron, who succumbed to idolatry
- Samson, a weak-willed womanizer
- David, the adulterous king
- Solomon, who abandoned wisdom for empty self-indulgence
- Gehazi, the greedy servant
- Jonah, a prejudiced prophet
- Peter, who denied knowing Christ in His most difficult hour
- John Mark, who deserted Paul and Barnabas
- Demas, the friend who abandoned Paul

Their examples show us that everybody fails to some degree, even ministers. So should we lower the standard, make it more "realistic" and attainable in light of our lifestyles? Should we cut some slack for our very human ministers? God doesn't, because His name, more than ours, is at stake.

---

5. Chuck Colson, as quoted by Swindoll in *Rise and Shine*, p. 225.

Unaltered Standard for Those in Ministry

In his letter to Timothy, Paul outlines the standards for Christian leadership:

> It is a trustworthy statement: if any man aspires
> to the office of overseer, it is a fine work he desires
> to do. An overseer, then, must be above reproach,
> the husband of one wife, temperate, prudent, respectable, hospitable, able to teach, not addicted to
> wine or pugnacious, but gentle, uncontentious, free
> from the love of money. He must be one who manages his own household well, keeping his children
> under control with all dignity (but if a man does not
> know how to manage his own household, how will
> he take care of the church of God?); and not a new
> convert, lest he become conceited and fall into the
> condemnation incurred by the devil. And he must
> have a good reputation with those outside the
> church, so that he may not fall into reproach and
> the snare of the devil. (1 Tim. 3:1–7; see also Titus
> 1:5–9)

Because of these lofty requirements, those desiring to become church leaders must carefully evaluate their lives and their calling as ministers. James even warned,

> Let not many of you become teachers, my brethren, knowing that as such we shall incur a stricter
> judgment. (James 3:1)

Christian leadership must not be taken lightly. Although God doesn't expect perfection, His probing eyes of judgment are more intensely focused on the leader—because so much more is at stake when a leader falls, as the tears of the innocent victims attest. To help you guard against potential devastation, here are four recommendations to consider.

Practical Ways to Avoid Doubt and Devastation

First, *refuse to deify anyone in the ministry*. Don't put leaders on a pedestal, no matter how gifted or capable they are. Respect them, appreciate them, acknowledge God's hand in their lives, but don't enthrone them. Instead, as you learn from them and follow their example, always keep in mind that they are fallible human beings like everyone else.

And ministers, don't accept hero worship. Instead, be like Paul and Barnabas, who, when the citizens of Lystra tried to worship them as gods, cried out: "We are also men of the same nature as you" (Acts 14:15). Allowing people to hoist you up on a pedestal may provide you a nice view, but it also makes you an easy target. It was also in Lystra that Paul's enemies stoned him (v. 19)!

Second, *remember that the flesh is weak and the adversary is real.* Jesus opened Peter's eyes to the evil one's lurking presence:

> "Simon, Simon, behold, Satan has demanded permission to sift you like wheat; but I have prayed for you, that your faith may not fail; and you, when once you have turned again, strengthen your brothers." (Luke 22:31–32)

Jesus' warning ought to make every leader shudder. For

> there is not an effective, gifted minister today who is not the target of the devil and/or his demons. Nor is there a minister strong enough in himself or herself to withstand the adversary's snare. It takes prayer. Prevailing prayer. It also takes being accountable, teachable, and open. Why? Because the enemy is so subtle. You see, no one deliberately makes *plans* to fail in the ministry. No minister ever sat on the side of his bed one morning and said, "Let's see, how can I ruin my reputation today?" But with the weakness of the flesh, mixed with the strength and reality of the adversary, failure is an ever-present possibility. Let him who thinks he stands, I repeat, take heed.[6]

Third, *release all judgment to God.* Anonymous letters expressing a critical attitude is not the way to keep a leader humble. Instead, encourage your pastor, get to know him personally, and, if necessary, lovingly confront a weakness, but leave the judging in the Lord's hands.

Fourth, *refocus your attention on the ministries that are still on target.* If a failed minister has broken your spirit, few words of

---

6. Swindoll, *Rise and Shine*, pp. 234–35.

comfort can heal your wounds or whitewash your memories. Grief may be your companion for some time to come. Our one word of advice is: don't withdraw into anger and bitterness. Rather, refocus your heart and mind on Christ and the positive ministries all around you. You can give again. You can trust again. You can have joy again, serving the Lord.

 Living Insights

It was career day in the local high school, and the teacher was asking the sixteen-year-old students to share their vocational dreams. One fresh-faced girl said, "I'd like to be a writer." A guy in the front row said, "Engineering for me." The kid in the back row called out, "Hey man, I'm just gonna marry some rich girl. Then I'll never have to work!"

Laughter rippled through the class.

Sensing an audience, he announced hurriedly, "No, no, even better—I'm gonna be a preacher!" In an instant, he was on his feet, waving his arms dramatically: "Brothers and sisters," he shouted, "that ol' devil has you bound up in the cords of sinnnnnn!"

The teacher vainly interrupted, "OK, that's en . . ."

"Amen?" the boy addressed his congregation, ignoring authority.

"*Amen*," chorused the students.

The class was his. "You gotta keep the devil on the run!" he exhorted, pounding an imaginary pulpit. "Don't give 'em your soul! Don't give 'em your time! Don't give 'em your money—speaking of money, I believe it's tiiiiime to take an offering!"

"That's quite sufficient . . . ," blurted the teacher, desperately.

The students roared with laughter, thoroughly enjoying the mockery.

If we had been visitors in this classroom, would we have laughed at the "preacher's" antics? Well, we would probably have chuckled a little; the show was relatively harmless. But behind the boy's flamboyant Elmer Gantry act was a jeering attitude toward the ministry that pervades every level of our culture, from politics to MTV. As Christians who love the Lord and His church, how do we respond when ridiculed? Our Lord was well acquainted with this problem—let's listen to His advice.

According to John 15:18–27, Jesus said that the world will hate us. What reasons does He give for the world's hostile attitude?

_____

_____

_____

Jesus cited two witnesses who will stand up for Him when the world is putting Him down. Who are they?

_____

Although we can anticipate ridicule, we must not cower from it. For the Lord is relying on us, with the Spirit's help, to testify on His behalf. According to Peter's advice in 1 Peter 2:11–12 and 3:13–17, how can we defend the Lord's honor before the world?

_____

_____

_____

_____

Remember, Christ never called us to defend the sinful actions of other believers, only to defend His name. Are you prepared to make a stand for Him in your world?

 ## Living Insights

"Five, four . . ."

The demolition team had strategically attached explosive charges to the supporting pillars of the old building.

". . . three, two . . ."

With a push of a button, the blast would shatter the pillars and the five-story building would collapse on itself.

". . . one . . . now!"

Kablammmm! As a cloud of dust billowed out of the basement, the proud brick structure looked stunned. It hesitated for a moment, swayed, then crumbled meekly to the ground. In a rush of air and dirt, the once grand building was reduced to rubble.

In a similar way, when an explosion of sin cracks a human pillar, the repercussions often demolish the whole building. Laying in the ministry rubble are those who trusted the fallen leader, who leaned on him or her for spiritual strength and guidance. Bruised and broken, they have difficulty trusting anyone again. They may leave the church never to return; worse yet, they may leave the faith.

Have you or someone you know become embittered because of a fallen leader? Has this situation caused you to turn away from the Lord?

> If that is true, I need to inform you that you are turning down the only perfect One who ever lived. [Whomever] you may be tempted to reject, don't reject Christ, the Lord! He is the *only* One who is absolutely perfect . . . the *only* One who can guarantee you a home in heaven. He is the *only* One who can forgive your sins.[7]

And He is the *only* One who can pick you out of the rubble and set you on your feet again. Please, keep on trusting Him. He won't let you down.

7. Swindoll, *Rise and Shine*, p. 237.

Chapter 14

I Said, "Send Me!" . . . He Said, "Go!"

Isaiah 6:1–9a

What does it take to win?

For the athlete, it takes strength, agility, and discipline. For a soldier, following orders, drilling, and self-denial. The winning musician must also do three things well: practice, practice, and practice!

What does it take for a Christian to win? In this study guide, we've set out to answer that question in a variety of ways. We began by anticipating the thrilling moment in heaven when we will receive our rewards—the crowns. Can you recall the five crowns and what it takes to win them? Here they are, listed in the order we studied them:

- The Imperishable Crown   Self-control

- The Crown of Exultation   Evangelism

- The Crown of Righteousness   Living daily for Christ in light of His return

- The Crown of Life   Glorifying Christ through suffering

- The Unfading Crown of Glory   Shepherding God's flock

In the second section of this guide, we explored each crown's requirements in greater detail. Now, in the final chapter, we would like to conclude the way we began section 1: peering into heaven. This time, though, instead of focusing on our rewards, we will be fixing our gaze on the Rewarder, God Himself. Our guide into God's presence will be Isaiah—the prophet whose vision of the Lord changed his life forever.

Setting the Stage

We know little about Isaiah, except that his father's name was Amoz (Isa. 1:1). "Some scholars suggest," writes Herbert Lockyer, that Amoz was the uncle of [King] Uzziah which, if true, would make Isaiah the king's cousin. Evidently Isaiah was of good family and education.[1]

Possibly, then, young Isaiah was an aristocrat—well-heeled and of noble lineage. And apparently, he was also spiritually sensitive, for the Lord saw in Isaiah the qualities that would make him the ideal prophet to the apathetic people of Judah.

According to Isaiah, his vision came to him "in the year of King Uzziah's death," which was about 740 B.C. Internationally, this was a secure period for Judah: to the south, the Egyptians were quiet; the steel-booted Assyrians were far away in the east; and the sleeping giant, Babylon, was as yet unaroused.

Meanwhile, on the domestic front, King Uzziah had busied himself expanding his kingdom. Although highlighted by many great triumphs, his reign had one black mark. Toward the end of his life, he disobeyed God by brazenly entering the temple to burn incense, which was the sole privilege of the priests, so the Lord punished the proud king by striking him with leprosy. Until that moment of sin, though, he was a good king, and the country thrived under his rule. His armies had pushed back the Ammonites and Philistines, extending the borders of Judah and opening up trade routes. As his treasuries began to bulge, Uzziah allocated his finances wisely, fortifying Jerusalem, strengthening the military, and investing in agriculture (see 2 Chron. 26). Indeed, this was Judah's golden age.

All looked well for the future too, since Jotham, Uzziah's successor, "did right in the sight of the Lord" (27:2a). However, affluence and security had hardened the spiritual heart of the nation, and according to the chronicler, "the people continued acting corruptly" (v. 2b).

"Prosperity often leads to religious neglect," comments Leon Wood, "and it did here in Judah."[2] G. Frederick Owen elaborates:

> There appeared extraordinary greed for riches among the men and fickle desire for fashion and ostentation among the women. Class distinctions became rife, foreign fashions were introduced, and the people

1. Herbert Lockyer, *All the Men of the Bible* (Grand Rapids, Mich.: Zondervan Publishing House, 1958), p. 157.

2. Leon Wood, *A Survey of Israel's History* (Grand Rapids, Mich.: Zondervan Publishing House, 1970), p. 354.

became so informal in their worship and so enam-
oured of the things of this life that Isaiah—the
statesman prophet—received the Divine call to de-
nounce in no uncertain terms the frivolity, laxity,
luxury, and vice so prevalent about him.[3]

That calling came in the form of a vision received by young
Isaiah—the man God selected to play a leading role in His eternal
drama.

Enter: Isaiah

As we enter the story, Isaiah has come to the temple to worship.
Suddenly, though, he is transported in a vision to the throne room
of God.

What He Saw

Recalling the experience later, he writes with a trembling hand,
"I saw the Lord" (Isa. 6:1a). Let's pick up this phrase and feel its
weight. When God called Isaiah, He did not give him a vision of
an apocalyptic catastrophe, the people's wickedness, or Isaiah's own
powerful future ministry. Neither did the Lord write on the wall or
arch His message across the sky in flaming letters: "I want you!" He
revealed *Himself* to Isaiah, and that is what changed his life.

That is enough to change our lives too. Indeed, unless we see
God for who He is, we'll never be able to really live for Him. We
probably won't have a vision like Isaiah's, nor will we ever read any
messages in the sky. But we can hear His voice in the words of the
Bible, and we can feel His presence in our lives. We can observe
His character incarnated in Christ, and we can experience His love
in other believers. These are some of the ways God reveals Himself
to us and arouses us with His divine wake-up call.

"I saw the Lord," Isaiah writes. "[He was] sitting on a throne,
lofty and exalted, with the train of His robe filling the temple"
(v. 1b). One commentator crystallized the scene: "The Royal Presence is everywhere."[4] Wall to wall, floor to ceiling, the robes of
God's flowing glory filled the temple and enveloped Isaiah with

3. G. Frederick Owen, *Abraham to the Middle-East Crisis*, 4th ed., rev. (Grand Rapids, Mich.:
William B. Eerdmans Publishing Co., 1957), p. 80.

4. George Adam Smith, *The Book of Isaiah*, vol. 1, The Expositor's Bible series, ed.
W. Robertson Nicoll (New York, N.Y.: A. C. Armstrong and Son, 1903), p. 63.

radiating splendor. He was standing before Almighty God. And he saw angels hovering above the throne and heard their booming voices.

What He Heard

> Seraphim stood above Him, each having six wings; with two he covered his face, and with two he covered his feet, and with two he flew. And one called out to another and said,
> "Holy, Holy, Holy, is the Lord of hosts,
> The whole earth is full of His glory."
> (vv. 2–3)

"Holy, Holy, Holy," those on the left cried out. "Holy, Holy, Holy," answered those on the right.

How many angels were there? We don't know for sure—the word *seraphim* is plural in Hebrew, so there could have been two or two thousand. Interestingly, *saraph* means "to burn"; these were angels of fire. With two wings the magnificent beings shielded their faces, with two they covered their feet, and with two they flew.

From the left they cried louder: "Holy, Holy, Holy, is the Lord of Hosts." From the right: "Holy, Holy, Holy, is the Lord of Hosts." The sound resonated throughout the massive temple, so that

> the foundations of the thresholds trembled at the voice of him who called out, while the temple was filling with smoke. (v. 4)

"The whole earth is full of His glory!" the voices on the left sang out, the intensity increasing to a deafening roar. "The whole earth is full of His glory!" responded those on the right, the sound pounding against the walls.

To us, the earth is full of enigmas and chaotic events, unfairness and corruption. It seems to be veering out of control on a course to destruction. But to God, the earth is full of His glory; He reigns supreme and is at work everywhere and in everything.

From the left, the angels raised their voices again: "HOLY!"
From the right: "HOLY!"
The ground shook harder. The building trembled as if it would collapse.
From the left: "GLORY!"
The right: "GLORY!"
The smoke billowed higher, engulfing young Isaiah.

What He Said

Hiding his face in his hands, Isaiah must have shrunk back in fear and awe. This was the God of his people—the righteous God whom Uzziah had offended with his presumptuous pride, the exacting God who was at this moment peering into *his* heart.

Unable to face God's holiness any longer, Isaiah finally cries out,

"Woe is me, for I am ruined!
Because I am a man of unclean lips,
And I live among a people of unclean lips;
For my eyes have seen the King, the Lord of hosts."
(v. 5)

"I am a man of unclean lips," he admits ashamedly, lumping himself with the rest of his corrupt nation.[5] This inclusion of himself contrasts with a long list of "woes" Isaiah directs at others in chapter 5 of his book. There he indicts the greedy rich (v. 8), the heavy drinkers (v. 11), the brazen scoffers (vv. 18–19), the unfaithful leaders (v. 20), the conceited (v. 21), and the morally corrupt (v. 23). All these woes he will direct to "those," but now he turns his finger of judgment on himself: Woe to *me!*

In the brilliant light of God's holiness, Isaiah sees his true self. How unworthy he must feel, his soul naked before the Lord. Yet unless he recognizes the depth of his sin, he will not discover true humility. And God will not be able to fully use him.

Then he adds, "I am ruined!" The Hebrew word for *ruined* means "cease, cut off, destroy."[6] We might say, "I am finished," or, "It's curtains, I'm done for!" Shuddering, Isaiah truly anticipates God's swift and terrible wrath. But instead . . . he receives mercy.

What He Needed

Then one of the seraphim flew to me, with a
burning coal in his hand which he had taken from
the altar with tongs. And he touched my mouth

---

5. Isaiah was no less culpable than the rest of his people, for he had the same fallen nature. And because he says, "I am a man of unclean lips," he may have even had a specific problem with vulgarity and cursing.

6. William Gesenius, *A Hebrew and English Lexicon of the Old Testament,* trans. Edward Robinson, eds. Francis Brown, S. R. Driver, Charles A. Briggs (Oxford, England: Clarendon Press, n.d.), p. 198.

with it and said, "Behold, this has touched your lips; and your iniquity is taken away, and your sin is forgiven." (6:6–7)

Incredibly, the burning coal of God's holiness becomes the instrument of His grace. As the coal touches his sin-tainted mouth, he feels, to his surprise, not searing pain but purging release. "Your iniquity is taken away, and your sin is forgiven," the angel announces. *Forgiven.* That word must have swept over Isaiah like a rushing wind, refreshing his spirit and relieving his guilt and fear.

What He Did

Then, for the first time in the vision, the Lord speaks.

I heard the voice of the Lord, saying, "Whom shall I send, and who will go for Us?" (v. 8a)

Can it be? This God of limitless power and mercy is *asking* for volunteers? He could have ordered Isaiah to serve Him; He could have shamed or manipulated him, but He doesn't. He calmly asks, then waits.

Isaiah doesn't make Him wait long. "Here am I," Isaiah calls out. "Send me!" (v. 8b). He has seen the Lord, lifted up and holy; he has experienced His sovereignty over the whole earth; he has faced the darkness of his sin and sensed the relief of God's forgiveness. Flowing naturally out of his grateful heart is his eager response: "Send me!"

Then God replies, "Well, Isaiah, you're pretty young. I think you should wait until you mature a little bit, especially in light of your problem with 'unclean lips.' You're going to need some education too, so maybe after a few years of schooling . . ."

No, God commissions Isaiah immediately and without reservation: "Go" (v. 9a).

Now Isaiah is ready to serve the King.

Exit, Isaiah—Enter, You

God is asking us the same questions that He posed to Isaiah: "Whom shall I send, and who will go for Us?" He waits to give the command, "Go!"; but He won't until we first say, "Send me."

Are you willing to say to the Lord, "Send me?" He may not make you a fiery prophet like He did Isaiah nor send you to a foreign land as a missionary. He just wants to know if you are available to

Him for whatever service He requires. That's the attitude of a winner in the Christian life.

If you struggle in this area, finding it difficult to surrender yourself completely to the Lord, here are a few questions with which to probe your heart:

- Is it that you have never seen the Lord holy and lifted up? The Lord probably won't give you a vision like Isaiah's, but He does long to reveal Himself to you in other ways—through worship, prayer, and Scripture. As Isaiah's vision teaches us, in order to say "yes" to God, we must first encounter Him in all His holy glory.

- Could it be that you are unwilling to leave your familiar and comfortable surroundings? They may provide you security, but think how much safety there is in the Lord. Material things will pass away, but God is always on His throne. There is no greater comfort than depending wholeheartedly on Him.

- Are you feeling too proud to commit your life to the Lord? Maybe you want to sit on the throne, reigning like Uzziah over your own little kingdom. One glimpse of God's holiness and power, though, quells that desire. Be like Isaiah instead of Uzziah, and humble yourself before the Lord.

- Is there some sin you've been hiding, unwilling to confess it? Let the burning coal touch your unclean lips and purify your soul. Then you'll know the true joy of being forgiven.

With starter's pistol in hand, God is anxious to shout "Go!" and pull the trigger. But He won't until we have lined up on the runner's blocks and said, "Send me." Won't you say that today? Then run the race with all your might—you know what it takes; now go on and win!

Living Insights

Let's spend some time considering those four concluding questions from our lesson.

1. Have you ever seen the Lord holy and lifted up? Perhaps in the past you encountered Him in a mountaintop experience, but maybe it has been a long time since you've felt close enough

to Him to experience His glorious presence. What can you do this week to draw back the veil of heaven and see the Lord?

_____

_____

_____

2. Are you unwilling to leave your familiar and comfortable surroundings? For a few moments, let the Lord examine your motives and desires. Are you allowing the security of things to supersede your reliance on Him? In what ways? How can you trust Him more?

_____

_____

_____

3. Are you feeling too proud to commit your life to the Lord? In what ways have you been reigning on the throne in your life? How can you keep the vision of God's holiness before you so that you can stay humble and dependent on Him?

_____

_____

_____

4. Is there some sin you've been hiding and are unwilling to confess? If you were standing in Isaiah's sandals that day, seeing the Lord in glory, how would you have completed his lament: "Woe is me, for I am ruined! Because . . .

_____

_____
                                                        "
_____

Thank the Lord that He touches us with the burning coal of Christ's righteousness and forgives our sins! Having experienced

His purifying power, are you prepared now to say to the Lord, "Here am I; send me"? If you are still hesitant, let Him know your fears. If you are willing to make yourself completely available to His will, tell Him so. The following space is provided for you to express your heart to the Lord.

_____

_____

_____

_____

Living Insights

Throughout this study guide, we hope we have helped you focus on your heavenly goals and understand better what it takes to reach them. As a concluding exercise before you get on with the race, review each chapter from the second half of our study and write down one or two ways you can make the principles you learned a part of your daily life.

The Imperishable Crown

Man's Disease, God's Diagnosis, Christ's Remedy_____

_____

The Importance of Judging Ourselves _____

_____

The Crown of Exultation

My Commitment to Christ's Commission _____

_____

Breaking with a Backyard Mentality _____

_____

The Crowns of Righteousness and Life

Gold in the Making _____

_____

Where Is God When We Hurt? _____

_____

The Unfading Crown of Glory

Doing Ministry the Right Way . . . for the Right Reasons ____

_____

Restoring Respect for the Ministry _____

_____

BOOKS FOR PROBING FURTHER

I f you would like to learn more about what it takes to win in God's eyes, we recommend the following resources.

Understanding the Crowns

Wall, Joe L. *Going for the Gold.* Chicago, Ill.: Moody Press, 1991.

Winning the Imperishable Crown

Ashcroft, Mary Ellen. *Temptations Women Face.* Downers Grove, Ill.: InterVarsity Press, 1991.

Eisenman, Tom L. *Temptations Men Face.* Downers Grove, Ill.:InterVarsity Press, 1990.

Winning the Crown of Exultation

Borthwick, Paul. *How to Be a World-Class Christian.* Wheaton, Ill.: Scripture Press Publications, Victor Books, 1991.

Campolo, Tony, and Gordon Aeschliman. *50 Ways You Can Share Your Faith.* Downers Grove, Ill.: InterVarsity Press, 1992.

Winning the Crown of Righteousness

Bridges, Jerry. *The Practice of Godliness.* Colorado Springs, Colo.: NavPress, 1983.

Peterson, Eugene H. *A Long Obedience in the Same Direction: Discipleship in an Instant Society.* Downers Grove, Ill.: InterVarsity Press, 1980.

Thatcher, Martha. *The Freedom of Obedience.* The Christian Character Library series. Colorado Springs, Colo.: NavPress, 1986.

Winning the Crown of Life

Kreeft, Peter. *Making Sense Out of Suffering.* Ann Arbor, Mich.: Servant Books, 1986.

Yancey, Philip. *Where Is God When It Hurts?* Rev. and exp. Grand Rapids, Mich.: Zondervan Publishing House, 1990.

Winning the Crown of Unfading Glory

Peterson, Eugene H. *Under the Unpredictable Plant: An Exploration in Vocational Holiness.* Grand Rapids, Mich.: William B. Eerdmans Publishing Co., 1992.

————. *Working the Angles: The Shape of Pastoral Integrity.* Grand Rapids, Mich.: William B. Eerdmans Publishing Co., 1987.

Some of the books listed here may be out of print and available only through a library. All of these works are recommended reading only. With the exception of books by Charles R. Swindoll, none of them are available through Insight for Living. If you wish to obtain some of these suggested readings, please contact your local Christian bookstore.

NOTES

NOTES

NOTES

NOTES

NOTES

NOTES

NOTES

ORDERING INFORMATION

Cassette Tapes and Study Guide

This Bible study guide was designed to be used independently or in conjunction with the broadcast of Chuck Swindoll's taped messages on the topic listed below. If you would like to order cassette tapes or further copies of this study guide, please see the information given below and the Order Forms provided at the end of this guide.

WHAT IT TAKES TO WIN

Olympic athletes share a shining dream: to stand on the top tier of the winners' platform and receive that highest of honors, the gold medal. All the years of strain and sweat and sacrifice and sorrow are worth it once that golden reward dangles from their necks.

Christians have even greater rewards to look forward to—not mere dreams but a reality as certain as God Himself. These rewards are referred to as "crowns" in Scripture, and they are God's way of making all our strain and sacrifice in His service worthwhile.

So come along with us while we learn about our eternal rewards and what it takes to win them!

		Calif.*	U.S.	B.C.*	Canada*
WIN CS	Cassette series, includes album cover	$52.64	$48.85	$66.35	$62.00
WIN 1–7	Individual cassettes, includes messages A and B	6.79	6.30	8.95	8.50
WIN SG	Study guide	5.33	4.95	6.50	6.50

*These prices already include the following charges: for delivery in **California**, applicable sales tax; **Canada**, 7% GST and 7% postage and handling (on tapes only); **British Columbia**, 7% GST, 6% British Columbia sales tax (on tapes only), and 7% postage and handling (on tapes only). **The prices are subject to change without notice.**

WIN 1-A: *A Look at All the Crowns*—Selected Scriptures
　　　　B: *The Imperishable Crown*—1 Corinthians 9:19–27

WIN 2-A: *The Crown of Exultation*—Philippians 4:1;
　　　　　 1 Thessalonians 2:19–20; Acts 8:26–38
　　　　B: *The Crowns of Righteousness and Life*—2 Timothy 4:1–8;
　　　　　 James 1:2–4, 12

WIN 3-A: *The Unfading Crown of Glory*—1 Peter 5:1–4

B: *Doing Ministry the Right Way . . . for the Right Reasons*—2 Corinthians 4:1–7

WIN 4-A: *Man's Disease, God's Diagnosis, Christ's Remedy*— Romans 5:6–11
B: *The Importance of Judging Ourselves*— 1 Corinthians 11:27–32

WIN 5-A: *My Commitment to Christ's Comission*— Matthew 28:16–20; Mark 16:14–16; Acts 1:6–8
B: *Breaking with a Backyard Mentality*— 2 Corinthians 8:1–9

WIN 6-A: *Gold in the Making*—Job 23:3–14
B: *Where Is God When We Hurt?*—Isaiah 41:1–10

WIN 7-A: *Restoring Respect for the Ministry*—Selected Scriptures
B: *I Said, "Send Me!" . . . He Said, "Go!"*—Isaiah 6:1–9a

How to Order by Mail

Simply mark on the order form whether you want the series or individual tapes. Mail the form with your payment to the appropriate address listed below. We will process your order as promptly as we can.

United States: Mail your order to the Ordering Services Department at Insight for Living, Post Office Box 69000, Anaheim, California 92817-0900. If you wish your order to be shipped first-class for faster delivery, add 10 percent of the total order amount. Otherwise, please allow four to six weeks for delivery by fourth-class mail. We accept payment by personal check, money order, or credit card. Unfortunately, we are unable to offer invoicing or COD orders.

Note: To cover processing and handling, there is a $10 fee for *any* returned check.

Canada: Mail your order to Insight for Living Ministries, Post Office Box 2510, Vancouver, British Columbia V6B 3W7. Allow approximately four weeks for delivery. We accept payment by personal check, money order, or credit card. Unfortunately, we are unable to offer invoicing or COD orders.

Australia, New Zealand, or Papua New Guinea: Mail your order to Insight for Living, Inc., GPO Box 2823 EE, Melbourne, Victoria 3001, Australia. Please allow six to ten weeks for delivery by surface mail. If you would like your order sent airmail, the delivery time may be reduced. Using the United States price as a base, add postage costs—surface or airmail— to the amount of your order. Please use the chart that follows to determine correct postage. Due to fluctuating currency rates, we can accept only personal checks made payable in United States funds, international money orders, or credit cards in payment for materials.

Overseas: Other overseas residents should mail their orders to our United States office. Please allow six to ten weeks for delivery by surface mail. If you would like your order sent airmail, the delivery time may be reduced. Using the United States price as a base, add postage costs— surface or airmail—to the amount of your order. Please use the chart that follows to determine correct postage. Due to fluctuating currency rates, we can accept only personal checks made payable in United States funds, international money orders, or credit cards in payment for materials.

Type of Postage	Postage Cost
Surface	10% of total order
Airmail	25% of total order

For Faster Service, Order by Telephone or FAX

For credit card orders, you are welcome to use one of our toll-free numbers between the hours of 7:00 A.M. and 4:30 P.M., Pacific time, Monday through Friday, or our FAX numbers. The numbers to use from anywhere in the United States are **1-800-772-8888** or FAX (714) 575-5496. To order from Canada, call our Vancouver office using **1-800-663-7639** or FAX (604) 596-2975. Vancouver residents, call (604) 596-2910. Australian residents should phone (03) 872-4606. From other international locations, call our Ordering Services Department at (714) 575-5000 in the United States.

Our Guarantee

Your complete satisfaction is our top priority here at Insight for Living. If you're not completely satisfied with anything you order, please return it for full credit, a refund, or a replacement, as *you* prefer.

Insight for Living Catalog

Request a free copy of the Insight for Living catalog of books, tapes, and study guides by calling **1-800-772-8888** in the United States or **1-800-663-7639** in Canada.

Order Form

WIN CS represents the entire *What It Takes to Win* series in a special album cover, while WIN 1–7 are the individual tapes included in the series. WIN SG represents this study guide, should you desire to order additional copies.

Item	Calif.*	Unit Price U.S.	B.C.*	Canada*	Quantity	Amount
WIN CS	$52.64	$48.85	$66.35	$62.00		$
WIN 1	6.79	6.30	8.95	8.50		
WIN 2	6.79	6.30	8.95	8.50		
WIN 3	6.79	6.30	8.95	8.50		
WIN 4	6.79	6.30	8.95	8.50		
WIN 5	6.79	6.30	8.95	8.50		
WIN 6	6.79	6.30	8.95	8.50		
WIN 7	6.79	6.30	8.95	8.50		
WIN SG	5.33	4.95	6.50	6.50		
					Subtotal	
		Overseas Residents *Pay U.S. price plus 10% surface postage or 25% airmail. Also, see "How to Order by Mail."*				
		U.S. First-Class Shipping *For faster delivery, add 10% for postage and handling.*				
		Gift to Insight for Living *Tax-deductible in the United States and Canada.*				
		Total Amount Due *Please do not send cash.*				$

If there is a balance: ❑ Apply it as a donation ❑ Please refund
*These prices already include applicable taxes and shipping costs.

Payment by: ❑ Check or money order payable to Insight for Living ❑ Credit card

(Circle one): Visa MasterCard Discover Card Number _____

Expiration Date _____ Signature _____
We cannot process your credit card purchase without your signature.

Name _____

Address _____

City _____ State/Province _____

Zip/Postal Code _____ Country _____

Telephone ( ) _____ Radio Station ____ ____ ____ ____
If questions arise concerning your order, we may need to contact you.

Mail this order form to the Ordering Services Department at one of these addresses:
Insight for Living, Post Office Box 69000, Anaheim, CA 92817-0900
Insight for Living Ministries, Post Office Box 2510, Vancouver, BC, Canada V6B 3W7
Insight for Living, Inc., GPO Box 2823 EE, Melbourne, VIC 3001, Australia

Order Form

WIN CS represents the entire *What It Takes to Win* series in a special album cover, while WIN 1–7 are the individual tapes included in the series. WIN SG represents this study guide, should you desire to order additional copies.

Item	Unit Price Calif.*	U.S.	B.C.*	Canada*	Quantity	Amount
WIN CS	$52.64	$48.85	$66.35	$62.00		$
WIN 1	6.79	6.30	8.95	8.50		
WIN 2	6.79	6.30	8.95	8.50		
WIN 3	6.79	6.30	8.95	8.50		
WIN 4	6.79	6.30	8.95	8.50		
WIN 5	6.79	6.30	8.95	8.50		
WIN 6	6.79	6.30	8.95	8.50		
WIN 7	6.79	6.30	8.95	8.50		
WIN SG	5.33	4.95	6.50	6.50		
				Subtotal		
	Overseas Residents *Pay U.S. price plus 10% surface postage or 25% airmail. Also, see "How to Order by Mail."*					
	U.S. First-Class Shipping *For faster delivery, add 10% for postage and handling.*					
	Gift to Insight for Living *Tax-deductible in the United States and Canada.*					
	Total Amount Due *Please do not send cash.*					$

If there is a balance: ❑ Apply it as a donation ❑ Please refund
*These prices already include applicable taxes and shipping costs.

Payment by: ❑ Check or money order payable to Insight for Living ❑ Credit card

(Circle one): Visa MasterCard Discover Card Number_____

Expiration Date_____ Signature_____
We cannot process your credit card purchase without your signature.

Name_____

Address_____

City_____ State/Province_____

Zip/Postal Code_____ Country_____

Telephone ( ) _____ Radio Station____ ____ ____ ____
If questions arise concerning your order, we may need to contact you.

Mail this order form to the Ordering Services Department at one of these addresses:
Insight for Living, Post Office Box 69000, Anaheim, CA 92817-0900
Insight for Living Ministries, Post Office Box 2510, Vancouver, BC, Canada V6B 3W7
Insight for Living, Inc., GPO Box 2823 EE, Melbourne, VIC 3001, Australia

Order Form

WIN CS represents the entire *What It Takes to Win* series in a special album cover, while WIN 1–7 are the individual tapes included in the series. WIN SG represents this study guide, should you desire to order additional copies.

Item	Calif.*	Unit Price U.S.	B.C.*	Canada*	Quantity	Amount
WIN CS	$52.64	$48.85	$66.35	$62.00		$
WIN 1	6.79	6.30	8.95	8.50		
WIN 2	6.79	6.30	8.95	8.50		
WIN 3	6.79	6.30	8.95	8.50		
WIN 4	6.79	6.30	8.95	8.50		
WIN 5	6.79	6.30	8.95	8.50		
WIN 6	6.79	6.30	8.95	8.50		
WIN 7	6.79	6.30	8.95	8.50		
WIN SG	5.33	4.95	6.50	6.50		
					Subtotal	
		Overseas Residents *Pay U.S. price plus 10% surface postage or 25% airmail. Also, see "How to Order by Mail."*				
		U.S. First-Class Shipping *For faster delivery, add 10% for postage and handling.*				
		Gift to Insight for Living *Tax-deductible in the United States and Canada.*				
		Total Amount Due *Please do not send cash.*				$

If there is a balance: ❑ Apply it as a donation ❑ Please refund
*These prices already include applicable taxes and shipping costs.

Payment by: ❑ Check or money order payable to Insight for Living ❑ Credit card

(Circle one): Visa MasterCard Discover Card Number_____

Expiration Date_____ Signature_____
We cannot process your credit card purchase without your signature.

Name_____

Address_____

City_____ State/Province_____

Zip/Postal Code_____ Country_____

Telephone (____)_____ Radio Station____ ____ ____ ____
If questions arise concerning your order, we may need to contact you.

Mail this order form to the Ordering Services Department at one of these addresses:
Insight for Living, Post Office Box 69000, Anaheim, CA 92817-0900
Insight for Living Ministries, Post Office Box 2510, Vancouver, BC, Canada V6B 3W7
Insight for Living, Inc., GPO Box 2823 EE, Melbourne, VIC 3001, Australia